The Charter School Principal

The Charter School Principal

Nuanced Descriptions of Leadership

Edited by
Dana L. Bickmore
Marytza A. Gawlik

ROWMAN & LITTLEFIELD
Lanham • Boulder • New York • London

Published by Rowman & Littlefield
A wholly owned subsidiary of The Rowman & Littlefield Publishing Group, Inc.
4501 Forbes Boulevard, Suite 200, Lanham, Maryland 20706
www.rowman.com

Unit A, Whitacre Mews, 26-34 Stannary Street, London SE11 4AB

Copyright © 2017 by Dana L. Bickmore and Marytza A. Gawlik

All rights reserved. No part of this book may be reproduced in any form or by any electronic or mechanical means, including information storage and retrieval systems, without written permission from the publisher, except by a reviewer who may quote passages in a review.

British Library Cataloguing in Publication Information Available

Library of Congress Cataloging-in-Publication Data Available

ISBN 9781475829310 (hardback : alk. paper) | ISBN 9781475829327 (pbk. : alk. paper) | ISBN 9781475829334 (electronic)

∞ ™ The paper used in this publication meets the minimum requirements of American National Standard for Information Sciences Permanence of Paper for Printed Library Materials, ANSI/NISO Z39.48-1992.

Printed in the United States of America

Contents

Foreword — vii
Brian R. Beabout

Preface — xi
Marytza A. Gawlik and Dana L. Bickmore

Acknowledgments — xv

1 Situating the Charter School Principalship — 1
   Marytza A. Gawlik and Dana L. Bickmore

2 The First Principal: Perspectives on Founding a Charter School — 9
   Marisa Cannata, Zaia Thombre, and Grant Thomas

3 A Culture of Caring and Engagement: The Case of School Leadership at Cedarlane Academy — 29
   Jeff Walls, Jisu Ryu, and Jason Johnson

4 Principal Change in an Existing Charter School: What Happens to Mission, Vision, and Culture? — 49
   Dana L. Bickmore

5 Transformative Charter School Leaders: Tempered Radicalism in Practice — 71
   Linsay DeMartino

6 Conclusion: Confirming and Expanding an Understanding of the Charter Principalship — 91
   Dana L. Bickmore and Marytza A. Gawlik

Index — 99

About the Editors — 105

Foreword

Brian R. Beabout

From their first incarnations in the early 1990s, charter schools have expanded rapidly to serve nearly 3 million public school students in the United States, about 6 percent of total public school enrollment (National Center for Education Statistics, 2017). This growth does not appear to be slowing, as bipartisan political support, aggressive philanthropic investment, and strong parent demand have led to continued expansion. This impressive growth has paled in comparison, however, to the rhetorical battles that have ensued as charters schools have called into question many long-held assumptions about American public schools, such as a belief in publicly elected boards and a strong role for districts.

Books on the emergence of charter schools have had some foreboding titles, including *The Charter School Dust-Up* (Carnoy, Jacobsen, Mishel, & Rothstein, 2005), *The School Choice Wars* (Merrifield, 2001), and *Educational Delusions* (Orfield & Frankenburg, 2013). Much of the think-tank publishing on charter schools has given more heat than light, and much of the peer-reviewed scholarship on charter schools has wrangled with the big-picture questions of achievement effects (Bifulco & Ladd, 2006; Zimmer, Gill, Booker, Lavertu & Witte, 2012), enrollment patterns (Frankenberg, Siegel-Hawley, & Wang, 2011), and impacts of charters on district schools (Winters, 2012). These are important phenomena to examine, and served as an important first wave of charter school research.

The book that follows makes an important contribution to what I see as a second wave of charter school research, one that treats charter schools not as a monolithic whole, but as what they really are: thousands of individual agreements between authorizing bodies and schools that intend to do things a little differently. Charter schools have been used as turnaround vehicles for underperforming schools, as niche schools that offer a unique curriculum not otherwise offered, as schools for students with unique sets of educational needs, and as schools that foster the linguistic skills and cultural identity of particular cultural groups. They have also, unfortunately, been used as a way to create quasi-private schools that use a range of hurdles to prevent the neediest families from enrolling (Renzulli & Evans, 2005).

Given this diversity, the most important question may not be "How do charters perform compared to district-run schools?" but rather, "How do charter schools serve students in particular communities?" The second wave of charter school research must necessarily be multidisciplinary, must be observant of the multiple goals the American public holds for public education (Rothstein & Jacobsen, 2006), and must always seek to view schools from the inside, as our students do. And this concentration on localism has important implications for leaders in these schools as they translate the external policy expectations into the curriculum, instructional practices, and staffing arrangements that create a school.

Leadership in charter schools must also follow many of these same guidelines, as the authors here illustrate splendidly. Charter school leaders must be multidisciplinary, as the typical principal skills of instructional leadership and building management must also be supplemented with good doses of entrepreneurial activity, financial management, marketing, public relations, and human resource management. Lacking many of the coordinating and buffering functions of a traditional central office, charter school leaders must be attentive to their external community, because their existence is predicated on parental preference, on navigating a sometimes uncertain political climate and, often, on philanthropic support.

Charter school leaders also must balance competing demands that emerge from the multiple goals we have of public education. Some charter schools have responded to these demands by shrinking the curriculum to focus on only some important goals, while others have developed unique approaches to balancing them. This is a core challenge for the charter leader.

Lastly, charter school principals view their schools from inside, because that is where their responsibility, and much of their influence, lies. While policy debates and media infatuation rage outside the school, the charter school principal is working from 6:30 a.m. until after sundown. The charter principal is often the subject of our charter school debates, but is rarely an active participant in them.

This text, then, comes as a timely contribution to understanding the specifics of charter school leadership. As with most issues of public policy, the high-level policy debates can feel awfully distant when the mundane realities of a school day are in full view. Charter school policy just doesn't have the immediacy of an unexpected fire drill or a teacher calling in sick at the last minute.

I work as a university faculty member in New Orleans, Louisiana. We are the city with the highest percentage of students enrolled in charter schools in the nation—soon to be 100 percent. So, I have a special interest in the success of charter school principals. Our program must meet the needs of aspiring charter school leaders. They will lead in unique conditions, many of which are described in the chapters that follow. As a parent and citizen, I would argue that it is imperative that the new structures we have rapidly put in place in the last 13 years are functioning. To build proper systems of preparation and support, the research base on charter school leaders needs to expand. This volume is a strong step in the right direction.

REFERENCES

Bifulco, R., & Ladd, H. F. (2006). The impacts of charter schools on student achievement: Evidence from North Carolina. *Education Finance and Policy, 1*(1), 50–90.

Carnoy, M., Jacobsen, R., Mishel, L., & Rothstein, R. (2005). *The charter school dust-up: Examining the evidence on enrollment and achievement.* Washington, DC: Economic Policy Institute.

Frankenberg, E., Siegel-Hawley, G., & Wang, J. (2011). Choice without equity: Charter school segregation. *Education Policy Analysis Archives, 19*(1). Retrieved from http://epaa.asu.edu/ojs/article/view/2779

Merrifield, J. (2001). *The school choice wars*. Lanham, MD: R&L Education.

National Center for Education Statistics. (2017). *Public charter school enrollment.* Retrieved from https://nces.ed.gov/programs/coe/indicator_cgb.asp

Orfield, G., and Frankenburg, E. (2013). *Educational delusions?: Why school choice can deepen inequality and how to make schools fair.* Oakland: University of California Press.

Renzulli, L., & Evans, L. (2005). School choice, charter schools, and white flight. *Social Problems, 52*(3), 398–418.

Rothstein, R., & Jacobsen, R. (2006). The goals of education. *Phi Delta Kappan, 88*(4), 264–272.

Winters, M. A. (2012). Measuring the effect of charter schools on public school student achievement in an urban environment: Evidence from New York City. *Economics of Education Review, 31*(2), 293–301.

Zimmer, R., Gill, B., Booker, K., Lavertu, S., & Witte, J. (2012). Examining charter student achievement effects across seven states. *Economics of Education Review, 31*(2), 213–224.

Preface

Marytza A. Gawlik and Dana L. Bickmore

The idea for this first in a series of two books germinated from conversations that we, the editors, had while attending the University Council for Educational Administration in Washington, DC, a few years ago. We pondered and reflected on how little surrounding literature there was on the charter school principalship, and the issues and challenges posed by the principalship. Fast-forward two years, and this conversation resulted in a symposium presentation at the American Educational Research Association on just this topic. Based on the positive response from this symposium, we decided to pursue a two-volume series on the charter school principal.

The first book in the series, *The Charter School Principal: Nuanced Descriptions of Leadership*, provides a foundational understanding of the charter school principalship through the lens of culture, mission, and vision. By drawing on the expertise of those in the field of charter school research, this volume expands our understanding of the unique challenges facing charter school principals as they engage in the core responsibilities of developing and sustaining charter schools. With this expanded knowledge, practitioners and policy makers are positioned to ponder and engage in improved practice, while researchers can further expand the knowledge base surrounding the charter principal.

The second book in the series, *Unexplored Conditions of Charter School Principals: An Examination of the Issues and Challenges for Leaders*, explores current policy topics impacting charter school principals. Drawing on sense making, teacher evaluation, succession, and socialization, this volume addresses relevant and new topics and challenges confronting charter school principals. It is our hope that this two-volume series will broaden and expand our understanding of the charter school principalship and make a contribution to the field.

OVERVIEW OF THE VOLUME

Chapter 1 provides an overview of the charter school principalship and our current understanding of charter school leadership. While the literature in this field is limited, we draw on studies that situate the charter school principal within a larger context of the important role of the principal. In addition, we present an overview of the charter school sector and current research trends.

In chapter 2, Marisa Cannata, Zaia Thombre, and Grant Thomas draw from a study on the process of founding a charter school. While many challenges facing charter school leaders are common to principals across school types, some challenges are unique to charter schools and, specifically, the process of founding a charter school. The authors focus on three such challenges: establishing and enacting a school mission; leadership and governance challenges; and attending to the business functions of school management. This chapter draws on interviews with experts who work for organizations that support charter schools during their start-up period through the use of technical assistance, training, and resources, and interviews with founders of successful charter schools. The data collection strategy was centered around Georgia, with Tennessee and Florida included as neighboring states with somewhat similar charter school laws.

In chapter 3, Jeff Walls, Jisu Ryu, and Jason Johnson explore the relationship between educational caring and student engagement. They present the case of Cedarlane Academy, an urban charter K–8 school in a midwestern city with a high enrollment of immigrant students. The authors examine caring and engagement in a school setting that scholars have identified as potentially problematic due to significant cultural differences between school staff and students. Walls and colleagues discuss the ways that school leaders intentionally sought to foster a culture of caring and engagement for both individuals and the school as a whole.

Dana L. Bickmore addresses how principal transition affects the culture of the charter school in chapter 4. Through the lens of organizational change, the author collected data over three years in a southeastern state to examine what happened to the culture of the school as a principal, new to the school, implemented his school vision. The chapter explores the connection between principal autonomy, change, and stability, and the potential downside of continuous change.

In chapter 5, Linsay DeMartino examines the use of transformative leadership practices and tempered radicalism as a mechanism to revitalize educational leadership. More specifically, the transformative school leaders at Millennium High School are "tempered radicals," defined as leaders who take deliberate and incremental actions that contribute to the dismantling of the status quo. Therefore, the purpose of this chapter is to investigate *how* transformative charter school leaders, as tempered radicals, operate and become community change agents.

In the book's conclusion, Bickmore and Gawlik provide recommendations for charter principals, those who manage and support charter principals, policy makers, and researchers. Each of these groups that impact charter leadership need to examine key questions surrounding what influences charter school leadership and how it differs from leadership in traditional public schools. Rather than focus on large school-level effects, researchers and practitioners need to uncover the "black box" of charter schools and determine what leadership practices are associated with better outcomes for students.

Acknowledgments

We dedicate this book to those researchers who explore and describe the work of educators inside schools. Through their efforts, we have a better understanding of how to improve practices that support student learning. We especially thank the contributors to this volume for their hard work and dedication in trying to open the "black box" of principal leadership in charter schools. We also acknowledge the support of the reviewers who provided valuable suggestions and comments that improved the content of each chapter.

Chapter One

Situating the Charter School Principalship

Marytza A. Gawlik and Dana L. Bickmore

Charter schools are public schools that are granted more autonomy than public schools in exchange for meeting certain conditions outlined in a charter agreement; these schools have become a significant part of the American urban education landscape. The earliest proponents of charter schools were educators advocating for school structures that allowed teacher autonomy to improve innovative practices (Budde, 1996; Shanker, 1988). This focus on teacher leadership and innovation soon shifted to include parental choice and improved equity as purposes for charter schools (Lubienski & Weitzel, 2010).

In 1991, the state of Minnesota passed the first charter law in an effort to infuse choice, innovation, and improvement to address parental dissatisfaction with traditional public schools. Minnesota's charter schools were the result of the state's long tradition of public school choice, which was welcomed by the state legislature and governors (Wohlstetter, Smith, & Farrell, 2013).

Wohlstetter et al. (2013) suggest that, since Minnesota's pioneering legislation, charter schooling has gone through three generations. In the 1990s, teachers, parents, and/or community organizations started the first generation of charter schools. These first-generation charter schools mostly targeted students who had not been well served by traditional public schools, suggesting that charters were mechanisms to improve equitable educational opportunities. Early charter schools established specialized curricula to appeal to at-risk students, to special education students, and to English-language-learner students. The second generation of charter schools, which span the late 1990s and early 21st century, sought to address questions of accountability, autonomy, and the effects of charters on district reforms. Advocates suggested choice and competition were mechanisms to improve school and student outcomes. State technical assistance centers were established to aid in the expansion of charter schools. Finally, the third generation of charter schools, post-2006, shifted from charter survival to charter growth and persistence, with a focus on how to improve charter quality.

The charter school sector has experienced incredible growth over these three generations, particularly over the past decade. Currently, 42 state legislatures, including the District of Columbia, have adopted laws promoting the development of charter schools. These laws have resulted in nearly 3 million students attending more than 6,800 charter schools throughout the United States (Center for Education Reform, 2016). In several large cities such as New Orleans and Washington, DC, charter schools now represent more than one-quarter of all public schools.

Five states—California, Florida, Arizona, Ohio, and Texas—host the vast majority of charter schools in the United States. Charter schools are concentrated in urban areas, which are home to approximately 53 percent of all charter schools (National Alliance for Public Charter Schools, 2014). This concentration likely reflects both need and demand. Educational reformers see charter schools as a means to innovate and improve on student performance in high-impact, low-performing schools (Lubienski & Weitzel, 2010).

Individuals are more likely to support the opening of charter schools in areas where student achievement is low and parents want more options. New Orleans, Louisiana, and Washington, DC, are the two U.S. districts with the highest charter school enrollment. More than 70 percent of students in New Orleans and almost 40 percent of students in Washington, DC, are enrolled in charter schools, and almost all the students enrolled in these schools are African American (National Alliance for Public Charter Schools, 2014).

The charter school movement is not without critics. Some have argued vehemently against these schools because they have not lived up to their promise of improving student outcomes and the school system as a whole (Ravitch, 2010), with some contending that charter schools have exacerbated issues of equity and increased segregation (Kotok, Frankenberg, Schafft, Mann, & Fuller, 2015). Diane Ravitch (2010) argues that charter schools have been usurped by privatization, and that the charter school movement poses significant dangers to the public education system: "The development of the past two decades have brought about massive changes in the governance of public education, especially in urban districts. Some children have gained; most have not. And the public schools, an essential element in our democracy for many generations, have suffered damage that may be irreparable" (p. 179). According to her assessment, the evidence base for scaling up charter school reform through federal policy and programs is weak.

Other critics, such as Jeffrey Henig, a professor at Columbia University, have commented that charter schools fall short in contributing to a more integrated public school system (Wohlstetter et al., 2013). As he points out, there was some hope that the choice model would lead to a more natural and sustainable integration at the school level. Henig argues that this has not happened, and there is evidence this may be true (Kotok et al., 2015; Miron, Urschel, Mathis, & Tornquist, 2010). Charles Payne, of the University of Chicago, further argues that there are significant geographic gaps in where charters are located, adding another layer of inequity in charter schooling (Wohlstetter et al., 2013). In short, Ravitch, Henig, Payne, and others posit that charter schools have fallen short of expectations when it comes to student outcomes and equity.

The focus of charter school research has been on policy, governance structures, and student outcomes, primarily student achievement. Little research has uncovered what happens inside charter schools that may support the practices and interactions that actually lead to student outcomes (Bickmore & Dowell, 2014; Gawlik, forthcoming). This is particularly true of what principal leadership looks like in charter schools. We know that leadership has an important influence on student and school success (Hoy & Miskel, 2012). Principal leadership influences both the school environment and classroom teaching practices (Bloom, 1998; Hallinger & Heck, 1998), and a principal's ability to establish strong, collaborative instructional practices is essential to academic success (Davis, Kearney, Sanders, Thomas, & Leon, 2011).

This book represents an effort to shine a light on an important, understudied topic in charter school research—namely, charter school leadership. We solicited chapters from some of the leading experts and thinkers in charter school research, asking them to examine the role of the principalship in the context of charter schools. What you will read in these chapters is a mixture of authors, with varying perspectives on charter schools, all grappling with the role of the principalship in the context of charter schools.

Contributors to this book include key charter leadership experts examining important topics such as culture and the construction of mission and vision among charter school principals. In the remainder of this introduction, we offer a brief overview of the importance of principals, and then move to discuss leadership in charter schools. We then examine the characteristics and roles of current charter school leaders.

THE IMPORTANCE OF PRINCIPALS

Reviews of studies conducted over a 20-year period conclude that principals' influences on student outcomes were primarily indirect, but measurable (Hallinger & Heck, 1996, 1998). The total direct and indirect effects of leadership on student outcomes account for approximately 25 percent of the total school effects, after controlling for individual student characteristics (Leithwood, Louis, Anderson, & Wahlstrom, 2004; Robinson, Lloyd, & Rowe, 2008). Further, studies suggest that leadership effects on student achievement appear stronger for those serving relatively high percentages of students qualifying for the federal free or reduced-price lunch program (Hallinger, Bickman, & Davis, 1996; Hallinger & Heck, 1998).

General practices shown to be important for principals include the creation of learning environments that foster achievement, which often involves focusing efforts on practices most likely to result in improved student outcomes, including the instructional development of teacher knowledge (Crow, Hausman, & Scribner, 2002; May & Supovitz, 2011). The knowledge base around specific skills and practices that principals bring to bear when influencing the quality of their schools is developing, with researchers targeting multiple areas for investigation.

Despite the burgeoning volume of research on educational leadership, what constitutes exemplary leadership remains elusive. Murphy, Elliot, Goldring, and Porter (2007) offer a comprehensive review of the research on principal practices (with a specific focus on studies of high-performing principals). They outlined eight dimensions of leadership practices associated with the knowledge base required for positive student outcomes.

1. Vision for learning
2. Instructional program
3. Curricular program
4. Assessment program
5. Communities of learning
6. Resource acquisition and use
7. Organizational culture
8. Social advocacy

These dimensions constitute the knowledge base required for effective school leadership. Keeping this in mind as we explore the practices of charter school principals is critical to assessing their effectiveness.

LEADERSHIP IN CHARTER SCHOOLS

It is important for the education community to understand leadership in charter schools for two reasons. First, charter schools are one of the most prevalent and rapidly growing school reforms in the United States. Second, the role of the principal may be different and more central to student outcomes and school change in charter schools than in traditional public schools, because of the greater autonomy and flexibility granted to charter schools by state law (Campbell & Gross, 2008).

The research on leadership in charter schools suggests that leadership roles and practices are configured differently than in traditional public schools due to the distinct governance and organization of charter schools (Hausman & Goldring, 2001). Several studies and reports have highlighted some of the unique challenges facing charter school principals (Berman, 2008; Campbell & Gross, 2008; Dressler, 2001).

Based on interview data, Portin, Schneider, DeArmond, and Gundlach (2003) found that principals of charter schools tend to have more autonomy and tend to allocate more leadership responsibilities to other faculty. Berman (2008) noted that in addition to serving as instructional leaders, charter school principals must "find facilities, develop and monitor budget and strategic plans, recruit board members, hire and train staff, recruit and orient families and work with governing boards, local communities and the authorizing boards" (p. 5). Successful charter school principals, therefore, must possess an uncommon set of skills, including both strong instructional leadership and solid business and management skills. Further, Dressler (2001) stated that the main purpose of charter schools is to provide parental choice, to reduce stifling bureaucracy, and to increase curricular and fiscal accountability while actualizing higher student achievement and parental satisfaction. In order to achieve these key outcomes, charter schools leaders must not only manage the day-to-day operations, but also ensure adherence to the mission and vision of the charter school (Dressler, 2001).

Campbell and Gross (2008) examined which of their varied and many duties charter school principals found most challenging.[1] The results indicated that principals have difficulty fundraising, managing facilities, and negotiating with the traditional public school districts in which they are located (while traditional public school principals do not struggle with these issues). In contrast, charter school principals reported that they do not grapple with mission or governance issues (Campbell & Gross, 2008).

CHARACTERISTICS AND ROLES OF CURRENT CHARTER SCHOOL LEADERS

Albeit limited, previous research has examined how charter school leaders perceive their roles and functions. In their examination of 17 charter schools, Griffin and Wohlstetter (2001) described four characteristic traits of charter school leaders. First, many charter school leaders came from outside the public school system, and had a history of challenging the "status quo." These leaders saw themselves as fighting an ill-constructed American public school system and often had an "outlaw" mentality. Second, charter school leaders expressed a sense of entrepreneurship. For example, some leaders worked to establish linkages with resources outside the district as a way to bring fresh ideas about teaching and learning into the schools. Third, charter school leaders were described as willing to work with municipalities to secure school buildings, teacher training opportunities, support for curriculum development, and social and health services for students (Griffin & Wohlstetter, 2001). Finally, members of the sampled charter schools characterized leaders as collaborative in their attitude toward teachers.

Carpenter and Peak (2013) explored how leaders in charter schools perceive their roles and functions. The authors posit that charter school principals described their role as fulfilling three specific functions: keeping the internal school community focused on common goals, managing staff members, and ensuring school safety. They also found that while contemporary research has defined instructional leadership as the hallmark of the principalship, in general, respondents did not prioritize responsibilities related to instructional leadership as highly as other responsibilities, possibly because in some charter schools the traditional principal role is split between an instructional leader and managerial leader.

Likewise, Cravens, Goldring, and Peñaloza (2011) found that charter school leaders spent less time on instructional leadership than traditional principals, in direct contrast to the assumption that greater autonomy should allow leaders to spend more time on instructional leadership. In contrast, Cumings and Coryn (2009) conducted a job analysis and found that job task statements were overly nested within curriculum and instruction. Thus, the initial evidence indicates that even though instructional leadership was deemed important for hiring purposes (Dressler, 2001), in practice it took a back seat to the managerial demands of the job.

CONCLUDING REMARKS

Scholars from education, sociology, political science, and educational policy have enhanced our understanding of the outcomes, policy issues, and leadership challenges that have emerged from the first two decades of the charter school movement. Although this volume is by no means an exhaustive look at charter school leadership, it does attempt to uncover prominent issues and questions regarding the nature of leadership practices within charter schools, a topic less explored in the current research.

To that end, we have included chapters from leading experts in the field to consider the impact of charter school leadership in critical areas, such as role of culture in changing and sustaining a charter school, and principal autonomy. All contributors were asked to consider the implications their research may have for the practice of and emerging trends in charter school leadership. In essence, this book aims to take a measure of charter school leadership as the movement enters its third decade in American public education.

NOTE

1. Although some charter school principals (typically those at schools in charter school networks such as educational management organizations or nonprofit charter management organizations) receive strong leadership support from a central office and are relieved of tasks that do not relate directly to student learning, the principals of typical start-up charter schools cannot rely on a central office for support.

REFERENCES

Berman, I. (2008). *Improving charter school leadership*. Washington, DC: National Governors Association.
Bickmore, D. L., & Dowell, M. (2014). Two charter school principals' engagement in instructional leadership. *Journal of School Leadership*, *24*(5), 842–881.
Bloom, L. R. (1998). The politics of difference and multicultural feminism: Reconceptualizing education for democracy. *Theory & Research in Social Education*, *26*(1), 30–49.
Budde, R. (1996). The evolution of the charter concept. *Phi Delta Kappan*, *78*(1), 72–73.
Campbell, C., & Gross, B. (2008). *Working without a safety net*. Seattle, WA: Center on Reinventing Public Education.
Carpenter, D. M., & Peak, C. (2013). Leading charters: How charter school administrators define their roles and their ability to lead. *Management in Education*, 27(4), 150–158.
Center for Education Reform. (2016). *Choice and charter schools: Facts*. Retrieved from https://www.edreform.com/issues/choice-charter-schools/facts/
Cravens, X., Goldring, E., & Peñaloza, R. V. (2011). *Leadership practices and school choice*. Nashville, TN: Vanderbilt University.
Crow, G. M., Hausman, C. S., & Scribner, J. P. (2002). Reshaping the role of the school principal. In J. Murphy (Ed.), *The educational leadership challenge: Redefining leadership for the 21st century*. Chicago: National Society for the Study of Education.
Cumings, L., & Coryn, C. L. S. (2009). A job analysis for K–8 principals in a nationwide charter school system. *Journal of Multidisciplinary Evaluation*, *6*(12), 157–176.
Davis, S., Kearney, K., Sanders, N., Thomas, C., & Leon, R. (2011). *The policies and practices of principal evaluation: A review of the literature*. San Francisco: WestEd.
Dressler, B. (2001). Charter school leadership. *Education and Urban Society*, 33(2), 170–185.
Gawlik, M.A. (forthcoming). Leadership knowledge and practices in the context of charter schools. *Leadership and Policy in Schools*.
Griffin, N. C., & Wohlstetter, P. (2001). Building a plane while flying it: Early lessons from developing charter schools. *Teachers College Record*, 103(2), 336–365.
Hallinger, P., Bickman, L., & Davis, K. (1996). School context, principal leadership, and student reading achievement. *Elementary School Journal*, 527–549.
Hallinger, P., & Heck, R. H. (1996). Reassessing the principal's role in school effectiveness: A review of empirical research, 1980–1995. *Educational Administration Quarterly*, *32*(1), 5–44.
Hallinger, P., & Heck, R. H. (1998). Exploring the principal's contribution to school effectiveness: 1980–1995. *School Effectiveness and School Improvement*, *9*(2), 157–191.
Hausman, C. S., & Goldring, E. B. (2001). Sustaining teacher commitment: The role of professional communities. *Peabody Journal of Education*, *76*(2), 30–51.
Hoy, W. K., & Miskel, C. J. (2012). *Educational administration: Theory, research, and practice, 9th edition*. New York: McGraw-Hill.

Kotok, S., Frankenberg, E., Schafft, K. A., Mann, B. A., & Fuller, E. J. (2015). School choice, racial segregation, and poverty concentration evidence from Pennsylvania charter school transfers. *Educational Policy*, October 1. https://doi.org/10.1177/0895904815604112

Leithwood, K., Louis, K. S., Anderson, S., & Wahlstrom, K. (2004). *Review of research: How leadership influences student learning.* Retrieved from http://www.wallacefoundation.org/knowledge-center/Documents/How-Leadership-Influences-Student-Learning.pdf

Lubienski, C. A., & Weitzel, P. C. (2010). *The charter school experiment: Expectations, evidence, and implications.* Cambridge, MA: Harvard Education Press.

May, H., & Supovitz, J. A. (2011). The scope of principal efforts to improve instruction. *Educational Administration Quarterly, 47,* 332–352.

Miron, G., Urschel, J. L., Mathis, W. J., & Tornquist, E. (2010). *Schools without diversity: Education management organizations, charter schools and the demographic stratification of the American school system.* Boulder, CO and Tempe, AZ: Education and the Public Interest Center & Education Policy Research Unit. Retrieved from http://epicpolicy.org/publication/schools-without-diversity

Murphy, J., Elliott, S. N., Goldring, E., & Porter, A. C. (2007). Leadership for learning: A research-based model and taxonomy of behaviors 1. *School Leadership and Management, 27*(2), 179–201.

National Alliance for Public Charter Schools. (2014). *The public charter schools dashboard.* Retrieved from http://www.publiccharters.org/dashboard/home.

Portin, B., Schneider, P., DeArmond, M., & Gundlach, L. (2003). Making sense of leading schools. *A study of the school principalship: A report prepared under a grant from the Wallace Foundation to the Center on Reinventing Public Education.* Seattle, WA: Daniel J. Evans School of Public Affairs, University of Washington.

Ravitch, D. (2010). *The life and death of the great American school system: How testing and choice are undermining education.* New York: Perseus.

Robinson, V. M., Lloyd, C. A., & Rowe, K. J. (2008), The impact of leadership on student outcomes: An analysis of the differential effects of leadership types. *Educational Administration Quarterly, 44*(5), 635–674.

Shanker, A. (1988). Restructuring our schools. *Peabody Journal of Education 65*(3), 88–100.

Wohlstetter, P., Smith, J., & Farrell, C. (2013). *Choices and challenges: Charter school performance in perspective.* Cambridge, MA: Harvard Education Press.

Chapter Two

The First Principal: Perspectives on Founding a Charter School

Marisa Cannata, Zaia Thombre, and Grant Thomas

Charter schools are one of the fastest growing forms of school, with about 500 new charter schools that opened in 2014–2015 alone (National Alliance for Public Charter Schools, 2016). This means there were 500 new charter school principals who had to establish and operate what is, in essence, a nonprofit organization, all while providing a high-quality academic experience and maintaining the support of parents, the broader public, and their authorizing bodies.

The initial academic success of a charter school is crucial. A national study of charter schools found that school performance in the first few years is a strong predictor of later performance (Peltason & Raymond, 2013). In other words, early excellence leads to continued high performance, and new charter schools with weak performance in their first year are likely to continue to struggle. However, other research suggests that charter schools often struggle with performance in the first few years, even if their performance catches up over time (Hill & Rainey, 2010; Kelly & Loveless, 2012).

Those first few years also bring enormous challenges—managing the budget, acquiring suitable facilities, designing the instructional program, and hiring teachers, to name a few. And though charter school founders encounter substantial autonomy in their decision-making as they operationalize their vision for a school, that autonomy brings responsibility for an overwhelming list of activities including, but certainly not limited to, maintaining appropriate accounting procedures; complying with local, state, and federal policy; providing meals, security, custodians, psychological services, and bus companies; and of course, educating children (Griffin & Wohlstetter, 2001).

School leaders have long been recognized as vital to school success (Leithwood & Riehl, 2005). Regardless of school type, principals are considered the learning leaders and drivers of instructional improvement (Bryk, Sebring, Allensworth, Luppescu, & Easton, 2010; Goldring, Porter, Murphy, Elliott, & Cravens, 2009). Principals have been shown to impact student learning by establishing a climate of learning and a coherent instructional program, focusing on school needs, and facilitating professional development (Day, Gu, & Sammons, 2016; Sebastian & Allensworth, 2012). Indeed, looking beyond the principal, characteristics of effective schools are largely similar, whether they are charter or traditional public schools (Maas & Lake, 2015).

The tasks that any principal faces is huge, including establishing and conveying the school vision, facilitating high-quality learning experiences for students, building professional capacity in teachers, creating organizational structures that support learning, and connecting with external partners (Bryk et al., 2010; Goldring et al., 2009; Hitt & Tucker, 2016). Indeed, this diversity and volume of tasks, in addition to the unpredictability of daily work, is a challenge that novice principals in traditional public schools face as they assume the heavy responsibility of school leadership (Spillane & Lee, 2014).

The critical role of school leaders and the heavy burden and unpredictability faced by leaders across school types is thus not unique to those starting a charter school. Yet, charter school founders face the additional burden of creating a new school without being able to rely on established procedures and organizational supports. Indeed, past research has called the process of starting a charter school similar to "building a plane while flying it" (Griffin & Wohlstetter, 2001). The leaders of new charter schools encounter challenges beyond those of traditional public school principals, and even principals of more established charter schools.

These principals face the challenge of creating a new organization and attending to all the operational and instructional aspects of this founding process. These challenges of starting a school are more pronounced in charter schools, as new traditional public schools face fewer struggles in the start-up phase (Kelly & Loveless, 2012). With these burdens in mind, it may not be surprising that turnover rates for charter school principals are higher than for principals in traditional public schools (Sun & Ni, 2016). The average charter school principal stays at a school for just under three years, which is less time than principals stay in both established and newly opened traditional public schools (Ni, Sun, & Rorrer, 2015).

UNIQUE CHALLENGES OF CHARTER SCHOOL FOUNDERS

This chapter draws from a study that explored the process of founding a charter school. While many challenges facing charter school leaders are common to principals across school types, some challenges are unique to charter schools and, specifically, the process of founding a charter school. We focus here on three such challenges: establishing and enacting a school mission; leadership and governance challenges; and attending to the business functions of school management.

Having a focused school mission is important for any school (Goldring et al., 2009; Leithwood & Riehl, 2005; Merseth et al., 2009). Still, mission-orientation is often cited as critical to success of charter schools (Cannata, 2007; Merseth et al., 2009; Wohlstetter & Griffin, 1998). Recent research has differentiated between nonprofit and for-profit charter schools, recognizing that mission-driven, nonprofit charter schools use distinct practices and have different effects than other forms of charter schools (Lacireno-Paquet, Holyoke, & Moser, 2002; Roch & Sai, 2016).

For example, Henig and colleagues (2005) distinguish between mission-oriented and market-oriented charter schools in understanding the role of school themes or target population, scale of operations, and student recruiting. Indeed, managing charter schools requires careful attention to enacting the mission (Frumkin, Manno, & Edgington, 2011). One way that the school mission plays a role in nonprofit charter schools is through the heightened focus on hiring teachers who believe in the mission (DeArmond, Gross, Bowen, Demeritt, & Lake, 2012).

A second area of leadership practice that is unique to charter schools are the governance arrangements. At the heart of the charter school bargain is the trade-off of increased autonomy for increased accountability (Finnigan, 2007; Wohlstetter, Wenning, & Briggs, 1995). In trying to understand leadership and governance in charter schools, researchers have focused on exploring how much autonomy charter schools have, as well as how and to whom they are accountable.

Overall, charter school principals report more autonomy over key decisions than do principals of traditional public schools, although actual autonomy varies by a number of factors, such as state law and whether the school was newly created or converted from an existing school (Finnigan, 2007; Gawlik, 2008; Wohlstetter et al., 1995; Zimmer & Buddin, 2007). Yet, charter school principals still struggle with having autonomy over key decisions (Finnigan, 2007).

Research also sheds light on how charter schools are held accountable. Charter school accountability and governance arrangements are complex, as each state has different policies about who can authorize charter schools and the responsibilities of authorizers (Wong & Klopott, 2009). In addition, charter school leaders may have conflicting accountability demands, such as demands from their authorizer or governing board and demands from market-based accountability (Blitz, 2011).

Authorizers vary in their ability to provide effective oversight of charter schools (Hill & Lake, 2008). As authorizers play a critical role in charter schooling by approving new charter schools, monitoring performance under its charter, and making decisions about whether to renew charters or intervene in struggling schools, lack of authorizer capacity to fulfill this role can lead to a break down in charter school accountability (Vergari, 2001).

Charter school governance also includes the creation of a governing board, although these boards also face several challenges, such as lack of capacity or training of board members and boards that either disengage or micromanage the principal (Campbell, 2010; Hill & Lake, 2008). Ultimately, lack of effective governance and disagreements among the governing board, principal, and authorizer can result in school closure and a negative impact on students and teachers (Karanxha, 2013). Indeed, one study found that 27 percent of new charter schools were disrupted by internal governance conflicts (Hill & Rainey, 2010).

A third unique challenge for charter school leaders is overseeing the business operations and financial management of the school. Most charter school leaders report serious organizational challenges, such as acquiring or managing facilities, and managing finances (Campbell & Gross, 2008). While these management challenges may be present for anyone taking on a new role, nearly 60 percent of charter school principals with prior experience as a school administrator do not feel confident in managing the budget and resources for the school (Campbell & Gross, 2008), suggesting the challenge is different than what faces leaders of traditional public schools.

Because charter schools, particularly stand-alone charter schools, are "school districts consisting of a single school," they must address many issues that are not relevant for traditional public schools, such as student recruitment, facilities, transportation, fundraising, and payroll (Frumkin et al., 2011, p. 95). Managing finances can be particularly challenging, as many charter school leaders lack the necessary business or financial experience, and may be why financial mismanagement is the most common reason for charter school closure (Frumkin et al., 2011). A study of charter school principals in California found they experience difficulty in balancing the instructional and operational/financial tasks (Zimmer & Buddin, 2007).

This chapter reports on the practices used by founders of high-performing charter schools to provide their new school with a strong start. By focusing on the three critical domains of charter school leadership, this chapter can serve as a resource for charter school principals, particularly the first principals of their schools. After briefly describing the data, this chapter presents the findings in three main sections that represent the unique challenges of charter schools.

The first section focuses on how charter school founders developed the mission and vision of their school and worked to enact that mission. The second section highlights issues of leadership and governance. The third section focuses on how charter school founders manage the business operations of their schools. All sections have implications for principals, and the conclusion provides additional implications for practice.

DATA

This chapter draws on two main sources of data: interviews with experts who work for organizations that support charter schools during their start-up period through the use of technical assistance, training, and resources; and interviews with founders of successful charter schools. The data collection strategy was centered around Georgia, with Tennessee and Florida included as neighboring states with somewhat similar charter school laws.

The first round of data collection included phone interviews with leaders who work at charter support organizations (CSOs). These organizations provide technical assistance, training, and resources to new charter schools and include local charter school incubators, state charter school associations, and similar organizations. The goal of these interviews was to obtain the perspective of individuals who have worked with a broad array of new charter schools during their start-up period, on what differentiates charter schools with a strong start from those that struggle to establish themselves and demonstrate high growth in student achievement.

We began by focusing on 10 states: Arizona, Colorado, Florida, Georgia, Louisiana, Michigan, New York, Ohio, South Carolina, and Tennessee, along with Washington, DC. These states were chosen because they had charter school laws similar to Georgia, or represented states with a large presence of charter schools. In addition to the state-based organizations, we identified three organizations that operated on a national level. A total of 20 organizations were contacted for interviews, and 16 organizations participated in an hour-long interview.

The second round of data collection included 90-minute, in-person interviews with the founders of 19 charter schools that had a strong start-up period. This included ten in Georgia, four in Florida, and five in Tennessee. All schools were created as new, stand-alone charter schools, although some have since formed a network as their school expanded. The schools were chosen on the basis of two criteria: expert recommendations, and independent verification of higher-than-average student achievement growth for the first three years.

Specifically, we accessed state achievement data to develop databases of charter schools that are not associated with networks or comprehensive charter management organizations, and compared the trajectory of student performance in the charter schools to both state averages and local district averages. When available, we also considered achievement indicators that accounted for the student population served (i.e., growth or value-added measures). After using publicly available test score data to identify schools, we used recommendations from local charter school experts to verify that the chosen schools were recognized as high performers.

The interviews were conducted with someone involved in the founding of the school. In most cases, this was the founding principal who was still the school leader. For four schools, the founding principal was no longer involved with the school. In one case, we still interviewed the founding principal. For the other three cases, a founding board member was interviewed. Most interviews were conducted with a single person, although in one school, the interview was conducted with a founding board member and the second principal, who was also one of the first teachers in the school.

Table 2.1 includes descriptive information on the charter schools in the sample. All schools were in at least their third year of operation, with the average school having been in operation for eight years. The average school had an equal gender split, although there were two single-gender schools, one male and one female. The average school was 52 percent black, 22 percent white, and 20 percent Hispanic, although individual schools varied in their racial composition. In the average school, 56 percent of students were eligible for free or reduced price lunch. Thirteen schools included elementary grades, nine schools included middle school grades, and three schools included high school grades. This adds up to more than the total number of schools, because six schools had grade configurations that spanned multiple levels.

FIRST THINGS FIRST: START WITH THE MISSION

A key component of any effective school is to identify a core mission and align programs and structures with that mission, although the mission orientation is particularly important for charter schools (Hitt & Tucker, 2016; Merseth et al., 2009). This was also true in the charters we visited. One charter school was focused on empowering young African American men to become productive civic leaders with a thematic approach that integrates experiences with aviation and aeronautics. Another charter school developed project-based learning experiences where creativity, arts, and leadership are a focus. Yet another school had a mission of initiating the young mind into the art of thinking through the teaching of mathematics and the Greek language.

Table 2.1. Descriptive Characteristics of Charter School Sample

School characteristic	Average	Min	Max
Years in operation	8	3	16
Percent white	22%	0%	80%
Percent black	52%	8%	100%
Percent Hispanic	21%	0%	84%
Percent FRL	56%	0%	98%
Percent female	51%	0%	100%

Note: N = 19.

Despite these differences, what was common across all the charter schools we visited was the way the mission and values infused every aspect of school decision-making. Why are you starting a school? What will be the defining features of your school? These are the questions that successful charter school founders spend a considerable amount of time unbundling. Every charter school founder that we interviewed was able to answer questions such as these in a clear and concise manner via a mission and values statement.

For the founders we spoke with, the purpose of a school mission goes beyond a focused theme, but has implications for core values they are trying to instill in students. Most founders described the type of student or citizen they are trying to create. For example, one founder said,

> So, you know we start with the philosophy, what do we want to achieve at the end of the day, who do we want our graduates to look like? And it is that learner, that critical thinker, the one that can stand up on their own two feet, know right from wrong, be able to add to society at the end of the day, and there's so many ways of doing that and not just the perfect A on the report card, which you will hear me say all the time that doesn't matter to me; grades are great, but who are you at the end of the day?

One founder not only described the school's core values, but provided examples of traits that, while positive, do not quite reflect the core value. This founder described one core value of collaboration:

> The way we define it is working together to solve problems, well, for a 10-year-old fifth grader, sometimes they want to give a shout-out to somebody for showing or providing collaboration, because they didn't have a pencil and you know, this person over here, gave them a pencil . . . that's kindness, that's good and props to you for being a good friend, but it's not collaboration. . . .

real collaboration would be like, you know, okay, if we were to equally—we're solving problems, again, together where we have this shared goal.

The founders we spoke with emphasized this specificity of the mission and core values to clearly describe what will be accomplished, how the school will meet its students' academic needs, and what differentiates this school from others.

A common theme among the charter school leaders interviewed was that the mission and vision were shared by all stakeholders in the school. The more concise and clear one's mission statement is, the easier the mission will be for others to understand and embrace. As one founding principal shared:

> I think the most important thing is the mission, the vision that the founders have. You don't make a vision a reality on the opening day of school, but the commitment to making that a reality has got to be there for everybody, not just for the founders, but for the staff, the families, and the kids. This is a joint effort. You can't do this kind of thing unless everyone is committed to it, and that's what I felt we had at the school.

While all founders described the importance of having all stakeholders buy in to the mission and values, there were a variety of ways that shared understanding of the mission was developed. For some schools, the mission was jointly developed by a founding group. One founding principal, for example, described how the school was established by a group of parents who began meeting because they were unhappy with their current schools:

> The local school systems around here just were not really performing very high academically, and it just was not a very good, safe environment either. So, a group of parents decided that they wanted to try to open up a charter school. And I was one of those parents and in the very early stages we just all, you know, really talked about what problems we saw in the, in the traditional schools that we had all experienced and the problems that we had experienced and what we wanted to see different. So, you know that kind of is how we started out forming our vision and mission for this school.

Another principal described how the first board president had the initial vision for a school serving low-income students that offered the same opportunities as elite private schools, and recruited the rest of the founders that aligned with that vision.

> The board that the president formed was pretty aligned to him. He called in a few chips. I mean, you know, I'm running a private school. . . . And I remember the phone call. I remember my foot was on a desk and I was looking out the window. I said, [Name], I don't know anything about public schools. He said that's all right. You know education. I trust you. Would you be willing to do it? And I couldn't say no.

Founders and CSO leaders expressed the importance of not only having a clearly defined mission and values, but ensuring that the mission and values guide decision-making. One charter school principal explained, "We make sure that our mission statement is not just something that's posted to the wall, but something that we are living and practicing and modeling, and then expecting of our students."

Those we spoke with indicated that everyone in the building should be able to not only articulate the school's mission, but also to articulate how every action and interaction in the school relates back to that mission. As one founding principal said, "Your values in founding the school keep those all fresh in your mind with every interaction you have about the school. So everyone that you hire, every family that you talk to about coming to the school, just don't go away or sacrifice any of the values that you were founded on."

Another founder agreed, answering a question about the school's academic program by going back to the mission:

> What's your mission, that starts, that starts directing you toward your curriculum that you have. . . . You've got to know what you really want out of this. What is your purpose for serving or doing this here, and what is your vision. And I think when you start there, that's when you can really build your program or decide your academic program.

Another founder described how enacting the mission of integrating refugee students into the community even had implications for operational decisions, such as transportation and food service:

> We'd have this sort of low-salt diet company that was coming in and feeding refugee kids who are used to a lot of salt and many of the pepper and chilis as well, you know these Burmese and these, these Middle Eastern people, and so the Africans did not like this very bland food, so one of the issues we had with them, is you've got to spice this food up a bit cause the kids are not eating it.

LEADERSHIP AND GOVERNANCE

Most founders in this study had experience in the classroom, and some had previously served as principals or assistant principals in traditional public schools. Yet beyond this similarity, their paths differed greatly. Some went through formal leadership programs, while others relied on their past years in schools. Some had prior experience working in charter schools, while others had only worked in traditional public schools. Two came from abroad. None felt they came in fully prepared to run a charter school. One founding principal noted, "There's really nothing that can prepare you for this until you're doing it."

Leaders repeatedly talked of "learning on the fly" during the long days and nights leading up to opening the doors and continuing well beyond the first year. The best preparation, principals said, was networking with school leaders from other high-performing charter schools—both within the community and across the country—to learn best practices and avoid having to reinvent the wheel. For example, one founding principal described his preparation by saying,

> I taught for four years before becoming principal. . . . I had completed a master's program in educational leadership. . . . I basically felt like I learned a whole lot on the fly. I went to visit a couple of high-performing schools. In fact, when I was hired, I was encouraged to go visit a KIPP [Knowledge Is Power Program] school [nearby] . . . that was one day of training for me, but I think that was as helpful as anything else that I experienced.

One reason why founding principals described feeling unprepared was the number of tasks that they faced. Founders and CSO leaders said that founding principals must wear many hats. They were the face of the school when recruiting students and communicating with external audiences as diverse as the authorizing body, parents, and the media. This was particularly true after the school was approved, but before the doors opened. As one founder explained, "I was one person masquerading as an organization. . . . I didn't have a director of operation the first year. You know, we weren't affiliated with the center. I didn't get a lot of money. . . . I wore a lot of caps. I definitely did." The founders we spoke with hired staff and recruited students, even while they worked with contractors to repair the roof and picked out furniture.

With the heavy demands and need to learn as you go, one crucial skill that charter school principals said they needed is time management. The schedule of a new charter school principal may vary considerably by the day. Leaders in this study recommended scheduling time during the week to observe classrooms, coach teachers, and interact with students. In other words, leaders need to make sure they prioritize being on the "ground level" of the school and realize that the school day continues long after students leave.

There were two key tasks that stood out as the most important for charter school principals. First was hiring the right staff. When asked what constitutes strong leadership, the answer that came up most often was the ability to hire well. Principals who are able to surround themselves with quality people and create a sense of trust are the most successful. As one principal said, "At the end of the day, success is for the people whom you lead. The whole idea is to lead from behind and let them celebrate their success." Another founder said,

It is key to part ways with people after year one as soon as you know they are not a good fit for the mission. Don't hesitate on this. Founders should hire slow and fire fast. Take the time on the front end to go through all the hiring process, but don't waste time if you know it's not there. You'll pay for it in the end.

The second key leadership task is establishing the school culture. For successful charter schools, culture is no accident; it is a fine-tuned vision that requires a great deal of forethought. One founding principal said, "we're very intentional about creating our culture so that it does not create itself." Founders described outlining what they wanted to happen from the moment students entered the building; schools would outline exactly what they wanted students to accomplish by the time they left, and plan backwards from there. No detail was too minute. For example, principals and their teams spent considerable time discussing how students would pass in homework, or fine-tuning the transition from one period to the next.

One founder described working with the instructional dean to develop detailed procedures: "It started when [the instructional dean] and I were on a plane, coming from a school visit. And we were like, okay, kids walk in the door. What happens? Okay, they have to go to a class. What happens then? Like, and then it just started really building from there."

When students arrived, the schools were apt to spend the first days or weeks orienting them to the school culture, planned norms, and expectations. Some schools planned thoughtfully around creating highly structured environments with silent halls and students in straight lines in order to develop a culture where students could succeed academically. Adopting another stance, one school created halls in which students could speak to each other and exercise their developing language skills. Another injected an element of socio-emotional growth into all student projects to create a culture of caring. The commonality among all schools is the focus on establishing a positive culture that fit with their mission and values.

One task of charter school leaders is to work with the governing board. As described above, founders worked to ensure that board members agreed with the school mission. In addition, founders said it was important that all board members be willing to invest a significant portion of their time in board participation, and to "roll up their sleeves." Multiple founding principals recounted meeting with their boards several times a week during the start-up phase.

One CSO executive said that founding board members should be prepared to devote at least 10–15 hours a month to board responsibilities during the early years of a charter school. Participants in this study indicated the ideal governing board has 7 to 11 members, each of whom is able to substantively contribute to school operations. CSO leaders and founding principals repeatedly recommended having a diverse board that includes members with the following areas of expertise: finance and accounting; real estate and facilities; legal and human resource services; fundraising; marketing; community partnerships; and academic programming.

One principal noted, "The founding board was strategic. We had our money people, our education people, a facility person, our construction person. Work, wealth, and wisdom . . . those are your watchwords . . . a school that wants to do good has to do well by guaranteeing that you have the people in place with expertise or connections to get that expertise." While it may be unrealistic for a board to contain expertise in every area, charter school leaders said it was important for a principal to complement his or own weaknesses with a strong board. One founder described the roles of the various board members and said, "Because I don't know everything—I didn't, as a matter of fact, I knew nothing about all of their respective areas, which is why they were on the board."

Founders and CSO leaders also said it was important that board members receive training on the distinction between school governance and school management, and on the respective responsibilities of the board and principal. One founder described working with the board:

> There have been a couple of times that I've, you know, had a conversation with a board member where I've said, "Okay, well that's, that's my job, and I'll take care of that." But, for the most part they do a really nice job of understanding that they're, they are governing and providing oversight, and they trust me to operate and manage the school.

Governance includes supporting the school's vision while simultaneously holding the leader accountable for student outcomes and complying with local laws and regulations. More specifically, board governance includes evaluating the principal, setting goals and creating metrics to measure progress toward goals, approving the budget, creating school policies, and fundraising for the school. Management tasks that follow under the purview of the principal include making curricular decisions, hiring staff, managing the daily affairs of the school, interacting with parents, reporting to the board, and implementing the board's suggestions and strategic direction.

The founders and CSO personnel that participated in this study made it clear that, while effective principals are critical, charter schools need to establish an identity beyond their founding principal. The average charter school in the study had been open for about eight years, and a third of them had experienced a principal transition. Two key themes emerged from discussions around leadership transitions: the need for continuity, and the recognition of special role of the founder.

First, it was clear that leadership transitions need to aim for continuity of the vision and mission of the school. When selecting the new principal, care should be taken to ensure the new leader understands and believes in the school's mission. In about half the charter schools that experienced a transition, the new principal came from within the school. For example, one founding principal described the person who replaced him as principal: "She was our first sixth-grade math teacher . . . she's been there from the get-go . . . it was a pretty smooth transition mostly because she knew the school as well as anybody." When a new principal was hired from outside the school, founders indicated how important it was to ensure a fit with the school's mission.

Most of the charter schools in this study had experienced leadership transitions in board governance. Indeed, all the schools had developed board succession planning procedures that involved a defined length of board terms (e.g., three years), with a rotating schedule of board member transitions to ensure there was not too much turnover in any given year.

The schools also had procedures to ensure continuity as board members moved on, such as having the board chair serve an additional year in a "past board chair" role or identifying the new board finance chair a year in advance so that the new finance chair could work alongside the existing finance chair. One founder explained that board member terms "are now three-year terms. They used to be two-year terms. I definitely think you have to be careful about the balance of getting new ideas versus some continuity of leadership."

The second key theme about leadership transitions is that, while continuity of vision is important, the role of a founding principal is different from that of the second principal. For example, one founding board member we interviewed stated, "By the time she [founding principal] was in the third grade, we realized we had an issue that she was fabulous for the start-up . . . there's no argument for that. But, as far as getting a school on, going from, you know, ground zero to maybe a little bit more cruising level, she wasn't the right person."

All principals experience unanticipated challenges, but the speed at which things progress in the start-up phase for new charter schools is accelerated. The second principal inherits a school that has a strong foundation, but is faced with maintaining and improving on that foundation. One founder mentioned the difference a second principal is tasked with: "You need to have some sense of predictability, some sense of consistency within your school day that you're just not going to all of a sudden be pulled here, or go here or there, or we're gonna try this. So, you need somebody that really can begin to calm and systematize the running of a school."

MANAGING BUSINESS OPERATIONS

While the founders and CSO personnel we interviewed described the importance of a strong instructional program, they also emphasized the critical role of managing business operations for their school. Charter schools are not simply educational organizations—they have significant budgetary and operational needs and challenges, and starting a charter school compares to starting any other major nonprofit organization. Managing the business side of the school is vital to its success. One principal stressed the importance of business operations by saying, "In education, we truly don't understand that it is a business and you operate as a business." Another founder described the importance of managing the school's budget: "The budget is your plan, and you need a good plan to get students where they need to go."

The founders we spoke with used various methods to effectively organize business operations, yet a common message was that the task of business oversight may become unmanageable for the educational leader (i.e., principal) alone. Most of the founding principals in this study hired someone specifically to oversee the business and operations of the school. Often, they began by hiring someone who had other responsibilities, but over time, business operations became the sole focus of one or two people. For example, one founding principal said,

> Everybody thinks all the money has to go to the classrooms and all the money needs to go to teachers. But I think the thing that kills charter schools is neglecting the business side of it. And that's why I so adamantly wanted a business manager full time, with an assistant. And we really have just gotten to that staffing level . . . finances will collapse a lot of otherwise successful charter schools.

Another founding principal said, "Your office manager is a key, key hire and I can't say that enough. I hired an office manager knowing that she would be our future director of operations. And she's still with us today and she's still, I mean, I talk to her about everything, you know, but you've got to have an office manager."

Another founder described not having a financial director in the beginning as a mistake:

> In hindsight, we would have gotten a financial accountant, manager, full time on the staff to balance those areas that a principal doesn't know about. And I wouldn't have had just a finance person; you have to have somebody that knows a little bit about facilities and bidding process and how to work with workmen, and stuff like that. So that side of the principal in hindsight would have been better.

In three of the charter schools, however, the founder took on the operations role while other personnel provided more instructional support for teachers, such as serving as an instructional dean. Regardless of the specific division of responsibilities, founders recognized that one person could not adequately oversee both the academic and operational aspects of the school, particularly as the school grew in size.

Founders also described the complexity of financial accounting and the need for establishing clear procedures, such as segregating responsibilities among three or more individuals (such as a business manager, board treasurer, and external auditor). Many founders said their own lack of significant financial experience led to their reliance on board members with financial expertise, or to contracts with organizations that provided back-office services. One founding principal said, "The board oversaw the budget, that was not my area of expertise, so over the years I had different people helping me with that, so we've had, like, business managers, bookkeepers, and for two years we had an educational service provider working with us in the back office."

The charter schools in this study developed a strategic plan with financial goals and budget projections, and we heard that board members with financial expertise proved particularly helpful in coaching the school leader through this process. After the initial start-up period, the budget for successful charters were self-sustaining on per pupil expenditures for core operations. Some charters created a finance committee to oversee the budget and to secure additional funds if necessary.

However, we found that while board members may be a great tool, professional staff was hired as well. As one principal said, "For many years, the finance chair on the board was the leading business person for the school. Well, you can't have that, because then they leave, and you get a less experienced volunteer, your business goes to pot. You have to professionalize it."

Another strategy for managing business operations used by many founding principals was to contract with outside vendors for various services, such as food, transportation, payroll and benefits, and janitorial services, to name a few. Some charter schools decided to pay the district to help with operations such as food services or transportation. Others hired local caterers or declined to provide transportation at all.

Founders valued the flexibility that came with outsourcing, because it allowed them to change the service if expectations were not being met or the needs of the school shifted as it grew. Indeed, many of the schools in this study described changing service providers or making decisions about insourcing or outsourcing services based on the quality of the service. As with any other employees, we found that operational staff were aligned with the school's mission and vision, and committed to student instruction and achievement. Some of the charters we studied decided to outsource some operations, but these decisions were made after thinking about how each business decision furthers the mission of the school.

A critical challenge in regard to business operations was acquiring resources. Principals and CSO leaders described the challenges of uneven cash flow, inadequate per-pupil allotments, expensive facilities that required unanticipated repairs, lack of capital funds, and minimal start-up resources. One principal warned, "If you're not terrified of spending too much money, there's probably something wrong."

To meet these challenges, founding principals and CSO leaders recommended focusing the budget on mission-critical areas, and establishing a reserve fund to provide operating funds when incoming cash is low. The principals we spoke with distinguished between the core mission-oriented components of the school, which they recommended taking out of the standard operating budget, and special programs that could be reserved if grants or fundraising efforts are successful.

One operational obstacle that was mentioned repeatedly by founders and CSO personnel was locating and paying for facilities. Founders noted that decisions about facilities were not only about the building itself; were also based on fulfilling the charter school mission through the neighborhood that founders choose, or by locating their building next to community organizations or higher education institutions with which the school partners.

Founders and CSO leaders indicated that the first building did not have to be the permanent location, and founders cautioned against exhausting searches for the perfect space. One founder said,

> I think the best advice I can give is to be realistic. Not to let your dream facility drive what you, your decisions that you make because, I mean, I could easily see a school not being able to make it financially if they jump into something that they can't handle too soon. . . . And I was like, no, we have to keep our sight on what's important and that's educating kids, and they can sit at a two-dollar desk in a trailer and learn, you know, better here than they can in a beautiful building at a school that doesn't have the, you know, the standards that we do for academics.

Examples of locations that our research encountered included churches, YMCAs, a music academy, a former car dealership, apartment buildings, an old Catholic school, and a college campus. Another common practice is to share space with other new charter schools or public schools with extra space. Yet founders continued to experience challenges even after securing a location. One founder described the tension in finding appropriate facilities: "Number one, you need facilities that are affordable, and you're not sinking all your instructional dollars into brick and mortar costs, but number two, our kids also need access to high-quality facilities."

Leaders we interviewed also advised new founders to be familiar with building codes, and understand that standards for educational buildings are more stringent than for commercial buildings. As one CSO leader put it: "There's no such thing as a free building. Charter school leaders really need a deep understanding of what it's going to cost to operate in the building, and have good real estate, construction, and operational advice. Unfortunately, that advice is typically something that a principal and school leadership team doesn't have." Many founders also said they benefited from having someone with construction or real estate expertise on their board.

Founders also described the need to treat the search for a location as a business decision, and recognize that building maintenance will need to be part of the budget. For example, one founder said, "Just be savvy from a business perspective. Yeah, and making them negotiate . . . just being really familiar with, you know, business tracks, tax credits available and, you know, community development, funding programs from state or federal sources, and vacant properties."

Several founders described how most of the unexpected expenses for the school were due to the facilities. For example, one founder noted,

> I can't think of anything that's been unexpected that, you know, has been so large that it would hurt us. But, I mean there are always little things like the roof in our, on our gym was leaking, so we had to have, you know, some work done to it. You know, if an air conditioner goes out, we have to fix it. They mainly deal with facilities. Most of those unexpected things deal with facilities.

IMPLICATIONS FOR PRACTICE

Successfully starting a charter school requires expertly balancing a myriad of events that occur simultaneously. There are several implications of this research for charter school principals. Each school is inherently different from any other school, and though there is no blueprint for founding a charter school, the guidance in this chapter is intended to offer practices that can be contextualized to fit individual school needs. By attending to the critical leadership tasks outlined in this chapter, future founders can lay the foundation for future success. For those just starting on the journey to opening a charter school, the leadership tasks outlined here can serve as guidelines for ensuring that founders think through how their school will address these issues, and how they will maintain a focus on the school mission while addressing these challenges.

For individuals who are taking over as principals of existing charter schools, these practices may also serve as guidance for maintaining and improving their school. During this transition, new charter school principals may want to review the leadership tasks to assess the progress of their school, and their success in addressing these common challenges. They may need to pay particular attention to renewing the school mission to ensure the school stays true to its founding mission as it expands and encounters the daily demands of education. If the evolution of the school requires a shift in the mission and/or vision, how will those shifts be communicated and support built among all stakeholders in the school?

Finally, these findings have implications for charter school authorizers. The accountability bargain that charter schools exemplify—greater autonomy and flexibility for greater accountability—place the authorizer in a key role for charter school success. Indeed, effective authorizing practices are important for upholding high standards in all charter schools (National Association of Charter School Authorizers, 2011). One essential authorizer practice is developing clear criteria for evaluating charter school applications. The guidance outlined in this chapter for starting a charter school may serve as a reference point for such criteria. How do charter applicants establish effective leadership and governance structures? How do they ensure effective business operations and financial management? Have they addressed how they will recruit and hire talent, manage external relations, and recruit students? If so, how do their plans in those areas contribute to fulfilling the school mission?

The hard work of starting a charter school begins long before the doors open on day one. There is no checklist or blueprint to starting a great charter school. Instead, founding principals must be prepared for the unexpected—all founders in this study described having to adjust their plan due to something that was not predicted, whether it was the local school district raising teacher salaries and making their own compensation less competitive, or a vocal parent calling attention to a particular procedure. The frenetic pace and competing demands will press the first principal in many ways. Again and again, the founding principals and CSO leaders in this study pointed to the importance of starting with the mission, and being purposeful about how every decision can lead back to fulfilling the mission and vision of the school. This is what it means to be a mission-driven organization. It is also critical for new charter schools to attend to business operations along with the academic program. Without a district office to take care of operations such as transportation and school lunches that traditional public schools can rely on, a charter school founder has the responsibility of handling these services. The founders emphasized repeatedly the hard work, cooperation, and dedication necessary to have a successful start to a charter school. Yet their pride and sense of accomplishment in being a founding principal made this effort worthwhile.

REFERENCES

Blitz, M. H. (2011). Market-based and authorizer-based accountability demands and the implications for charter school leadership. *Journal of School Choice, 5*(4), 357–396. https://doi.org/10.1080/15582159.2011.624911

Bryk, A. S., Sebring, P. B., Allensworth, E., Luppescu, S., & Easton, J. Q. (2010). *Organizing schools for improvement: Lessons from Chicago*. Chicago: University of Chicago Press.

Campbell, C. (2010). *Missed opportunity: Improving charter school governing boards*. Seattle, WA: Center for Reinventing Public Education. Retrieved from http://www.crpe.org/publications/ch-6-missed-opportunity-improving-charter-school-governing-boards-hfr-09

Campbell, C., & Gross, B. (2008). *Working without a safety net: How charter school leaders can best survive on the high wire*. Seattle, WA: Center for Reinventing Public Education.

Cannata, M. (2007). Teacher community and elementary charter schools. *Education Policy Analysis Archives, 15*(11). Retrieved from http://epaa.asu.edu/epaa/v15n11/

Day, C., Gu, Q., & Sammons, P. (2016). The impact of leadership on student outcomes: How successful school leaders use transformational and instructional strategies to make a difference. *Educational Administration Quarterly, 52*(2), 221–258. https://doi.org/10.1177/0013161X15616863

DeArmond, M., Gross, B., Bowen, M., Demeritt, A., & Lake, R. (2012). *Managing talent for school coherence: Learning from charter management organizations*. Seattle, WA: Center on Reinventing Public Education. Retrieved from http://www.crpe.org/publications/managing-talent-school-coherence-learning-charter-management-organizations

Finnigan, K. S. (2007). Charter school autonomy: The mismatch between theory and practice. *Educational Policy, 21*, 503–526.

Frumkin, P., Manno, B. V., & Edgington, N. (2011). *The strategic management of charter schools: Frameworks and tools for educational entrepreneurs*. Cambridge, MA: Harvard Education Press.

Gawlik, M. A. (2008). Breaking loose: Principal autonomy in charter and public schools. *Educational Policy, 22*(6), 783–804. https://doi.org/10.1177/0895904807307058

Goldring, E., Porter, A., Murphy, J., Elliott, S. N., & Cravens, X. (2009). Assessing learning-centered leadership: Connections to research, professional standards, and current practices. *Leadership and Policy in Schools, 8*(1), 1–36.

Griffin, N. C., & Wohlstetter, P. (2001). Building a plane while flying it: Early lessons from developing charter schools. *Teachers College Record, 103*(2), 336–365.

Henig, J. R., Holyoke, T. T., Brown, H., & Lacireno-Paquet, N. (2005). The influence of founder type on charter school structures and operations. *American Journal of Education, 111*(4), 487–522.

Hill, P. T., & Lake, R. J. (2008). Charter school governance. In M. Berends, M. Springer, & H. J. Walberg (Eds.), *Charter school outcomes* (pp. 113–129). New York: Lawrence Erlbaum Associates.

Hill, P. T., & Rainey, L. (2010). Charter school maturation as a factor in performance assessment and accountability. In J. R. Betts & P. T. Hill (Eds.), *Taking measure of charter schools: better assessments, better policymaking, better schools* (pp. 113–128). Lanham, MD: Rowman & Littlefield Education.

Hitt, D. H., & Tucker, P. D. (2016). Systematic review of key leader practices found to influence student achievement: A unified framework. *Review of Educational Research, 86*(2), 531–569. https://doi.org/10.3102/0034654315614911

Karanxha, Z. (2013). When the "dream" turns into a nightmare: Life and death of voyager charter school. *Educational Administration Quarterly, 49*(4), 576–609. https://doi.org/10.1177/0013161X12471832

Kelly, A. P., & Loveless, T. (2012). Comparing new school effects in charter and traditional public schools. *American Journal of Education, 118*(4), 427–453. https://doi.org/10.1086/666370

Lacireno-Paquet, N., Holyoke, T. T., & Moser, M. (2002). Creaming versus cropping: Charter school enrollment practices in response to market incentives. *Educational Evaluation and Policy Analysis, 24*(2), 145–158.

Leithwood, K., & Riehl, C. (2005). What do we know about successful school leadership. In W. A. Firestone & C. Riehl (Eds.), *A new agenda: Directions for research on educational leadership* (pp. 12–27). New York: Teachers College Press.

Maas, T., & Lake, R. (2015). Effective charter and traditional school characteristics: Aligning findings for informed policy making. *Journal of School Choice, 9*(2), 165–178. https://doi.org/10.1080/15582159.2015.1028311

Merseth, K. K., Cooper, K., Roberts, J., Tieken, M. C., Valant, J., & Wynne, C. (2009). *Inside urban charter schools: Promising practices and strategies in five high-performing schools.* Cambridge, MA: Harvard Education Press.

National Alliance for Public Charter Schools. (2016). Charter school data dashboard. Retrieved from http://dashboard2.publiccharters.org/National/

National Association of Charter School Authorizers. (2011). *Spotlight on essential practices.* Chicago: National Association of Charter School Authorizers.

Ni, Y., Sun, M., & Rorrer, A. (2015). Principal turnover upheaval and uncertainty in charter schools? *Educational Administration Quarterly, 51*(3), 409–437. https://doi.org/10.1177/0013161X14539808

Peltason, E. H., & Raymond, M. E. (2013). *Charter school growth and replication, volume 1.* Stanford, CA: Center for Research on Education Outcomes. Retrieved from http://credo.stanford.edu/documents/CGARGrowthVolumeIN.pdf

Roch, C. H., & Sai, N. (2016). Charter school teacher job satisfaction. *Educational Policy*, January 10. https://doi.org/10.1177/0895904815625281

Sebastian, J., & Allensworth, E. (2012). The influence of principal leadership on classroom instruction and student learning: A study of mediated pathways to learning. *Educational Administration Quarterly, 48*(4), 626–663. https://doi.org/10.1177/0013161X11436273

Spillane, J. P., & Lee, L. C. (2014). Novice school principals' sense of ultimate responsibility: Problems of practice in transitioning to the principal's office. *Educational Administration Quarterly, 50*(3), 431–465. https://doi.org/10.1177/0013161X13505290

Sun, M., & Ni, Y. (2016). Work environments and labor markets explaining principal turnover gap between charter schools and traditional public schools. *Educational Administration Quarterly, 52*(1), 144–183. https://doi.org/10.1177/0013161X15616659

Vergari, S. (2001). Charter school authorizes public agents for holding charter schools accountable. *Education and Urban Society, 33*(2), 129–140. https://doi.org/10.1177/0013124501332003

Wohlstetter, P., & Griffin, N. (1998). *Creating and sustaining learning communities: Early lessons from charter schools.* Philadelphia: Consortium for Policy Research in Education, University of Pennsylvania.

Wohlstetter, P., Wenning, R., & Briggs, K. L. (1995). Charter schools in the United States: The question of autonomy. *Educational Policy, 9*(4), 331–359.

Wong, K. K., & Klopott, S. (2009). Politics and governance in charter schools. In M. Berends, M. G. Springer, D. Ballou, & H. J. Walberg (Eds.), *Handbook of research on school choice* (pp. 115–135). New York: Routledge.

Zimmer, R., & Buddin, R. (2007). Getting inside the black box: Examining how the operation of charter schools affects performance. *Peabody Journal of Education, 82*(2), 43.

Chapter Three

A Culture of Caring and Engagement

The Case of School Leadership at Cedarlane Academy

Jeff Walls, Jisu Ryu, and Jason Johnson

Leading a charter school is often a delicate balancing act. Over the past two decades, through initiatives such as No Child Left Behind and Race to the Top, the federal government has pushed states to pursue evidence-based strategies to improve student achievement. One response has been the creation of public charter schools that are marked by a heavy emphasis on accountability and raising academic standards. In some urban areas, many of these schools are marketed to (or have attracted) many students from recent immigrant families, which results in a diverse and highly multicultural population.

The teaching staff, however, is more typical of the teaching force as a whole: white, middle class, and often early in their career (Darling-Hammond & Sclan, 1996). Leaders in these schools must, therefore, negotiate a wide variety of expectations from very different constituencies: authorizing agencies, parents, students, and teachers.

One of the most pressing challenges facing these school leaders is how to design a school that transcends cultural differences in order to provide a supportive environment for all students while simultaneously producing high performance on state tests that often disadvantage immigrant students in a variety of ways. Despite the current emphasis on academic accountability, previous research has found that schools characterized by a balance of academic press with strong academic and social support benefit students the most in terms of academic achievement, as well as their personal well-being (Ancess, 2000; Lee & Smith, 1999; Marks, 2000).

Achieving the appropriate balance is not unproblematic, particularly in a multicultural school where families and students bring with them a wide variety of expectations about what constitutes both rigor and support. The imperative for finding effective ways to educate immigrant students is growing more acute as the proportion of students born outside the United States continues to grow. Parents, policy makers, school leaders, and researchers are interested in how best to achieve this equilibrium.

The present study examines how the school leaders at one school approached the dilemma of balancing support and press. We explore the case of Cedarlane Academy, an urban charter K–8 school in a midwestern city. Cedarlane Academy is a particularly fertile ground to examine the above dilemma, because the student body is composed almost entirely of first- or 1.5-generation immigrants, mostly from North and East Africa (though hailing from several ethnicities and cultural traditions within that region). Like most schools in the state, teaching staff and administration are composed mostly of white women and a few white men.

Importantly, student achievement at Cedarlane Academy is considerably higher than in the surrounding school district, as measured by state standardized tests. This investigation focuses particularly on two concepts—caring and student engagement—with the intention of understanding the links between the concepts as well as how the school leaders at Cedarlane Academy generated a transcultural ethic of care complemented by high student engagement.

THE PROBLEM OF CARING

Philosopher Nel Noddings is the most frequently cited theorist whose writing explicitly focuses on caring and education. Noddings's (1992, 2005, 2006, 2013) philosophy is rooted in a feminine ethic of care: good caring in schools is essentially familial in its orientation. Noddings (2005) posits several important characteristics of caring. First, for an action to be truly caring, the person cared for must recognize it as such. Second, caring actions are responding to needs, and educators must balance competing needs in caring for children (e.g., the need for a student to talk to peers with the need for a student to listen to instructions on how to complete an activity). Noddings's view of caring is rooted in relationships, intent, and recognition.

Critiques of Noddings's conceptualization have come from two directions. Tronto (2010), a political philosopher, critiques the conceptualization of caring by noting that organizational caring is different than the familial ethic of care in which Noddings's formulation is rooted. Tronto highlights three aspects of care that organizations ought to intentionally examine to ethically undergird the basis of care: the purpose of care, the particular care needed by individuals, and the power relationships that mediate care (and differences in how care is intended and received).

The introduction of power into the "familial model" of care is particularly important when extending Noddings's work to upper elementary grades or secondary schools, where students have more independence than their very young counterparts (Hargreaves, Earl, & Ryan, 1996).

Second, Thompson (1998) and other critical scholars point out that not all students and families practice or experience caring in the same way, particularly with respect to communities of color (see also Epstein, 2001). For Thompson, Noddings's notion of care focuses too narrowly on the experiences of white, middle-class women teaching white, middle-class students. For students with different experiences and different cultural backgrounds, Noddings's way of thinking about caring may or may not apply.

These fissures on the nature of caring in education are present in the empirical literature as well as the theoretical. Victor Battistich and colleagues found that caring school communities are associated with better attitudes, higher motivation, and better behavior for students (and, to a lesser extent, to better academic outcomes) (Battistich, Solomon, Kim, Watson, & Schaps, 1995; Battistich, Solomon, Watson, & Schaps, 1997).

Other scholars have challenged the way that caring is operationalized in schools. Hoffman (2009) notes,

> The caring community, when translated into practice, becomes a discourse about activities and behaviors teachers get children to engage in. . . . What is essentially happening is that when it comes to describing and recommending actual practices of classroom management, the language of caring ideals often devolves to a discourse about control, rules, contracts, choices, activities, and organizational structures. In effect, substance is replaced by structure; feeling is replaced by form. Most tellingly, caring and community are conceptualized as things teachers teach children to do by getting them to behave in appropriate ways. . . . Caring and community become lessons taught by teachers to children rather than deeply felt shared emotions embedded in the human relationships of the classroom. (p. 545)

Some scholars have argued that this form of caring, as practiced in traditional public schools, divests students from non-white, non-middle-class families of social and cultural capital by imposing assimilation and dismissing students' own notions of education (Antrop-González & De Jesús, 2006; Bartlett & García, 2011; Duncan-Andrade, 2007, 2009; Rolón-Dow, 2005; Valenzuela, 1999). These scholars, in effect, critique the way that caring is enacted in schools.

Caring is thus problematic in education. Scholars agree that caring in schools is associated with higher levels of student engagement (Antrop-González & De Jesús, 2006; Marks, 2000; Wentzel, 1997), greater social and emotional learning (Battistich et al., 1995; Durlak, Weissberg, & Pachan, 2010), and stronger sense of belonging in both school and community

(McKamey, 2011; Riley, 2013b). However, many students, and especially students exposed to opportunity gaps, do not experience schools as caring places (Duncan-Andrade, 2009; Riley, 2013a; Valenzuela, 1999), and this may increase disengagement from school.

Valenzuela (1999) in particular links problematic forms of caring to student engagement. In an ethnographic study, she disentangles how teachers, who say they care deeply about their students, act in ways that divorce school knowledge from the culture and cultural knowledge that the students bring with them to school. The result is that students become disaffected and disengaged. Although multiple caring scholars find that effective care for students boosts engagement (and vice versa), there has been little systematic effort to deepen our understanding of this relationship and how it impacts students.

THE PROBLEM OF ENGAGEMENT

While most scholars agree that student engagement has multiple dimensions, there is a lack of consensus on what those dimensions are, and how they are measured. Reschly and Christenson (2012) refer to this phenomenon as jingle—"same term is used to refer to different things," and jangle—"different terms are used for the same construct" (p. 11). There exist numerous models of student engagement, comprised of two, three, or even four dimensions. In short, though there are a plethora of options for measuring student engagement, there is also considerable murkiness surrounding the concept.

Lawson and Lawson (2013) begin to frame student engagement in a different way. They suggest that "exploring how the study of student engagement dispositions, population characteristics, school ecologies, and place-based, social geography might better highlight the engagement-related strengths and needs of vulnerable student populations" (p. 434). The authors argue that developing an understanding for the way students engage in the classroom is insufficient.

Rather, we must conceptualize engagement as a social ecological framework that encompasses the degree and type of student engagement, not only in classrooms, but in school and community more broadly. The interplay between classroom and community engagement, the authors suggest, may help school leaders and policy makers to design strategies for engagement that better reflect the entire continuum of student experiences.

The conceptual gap that Lawson and Lawson (2013) identify in the student engagement literature suggests room for more explicitly marrying the literatures on educational caring and student engagement, as well as room for growth in both literatures. In the same way that the engagement literature to date largely focuses on student engagement in classroom or academic activities, the literature on educational caring tends to consist mostly in consideration of the student-teacher relationship. Although relationships are central to both caring and engagement, these relationships are mediated in important ways by the broader school and community setting.

A CULTURE OF CARING AND ENGAGEMENT

One significant shortcoming in the literatures on both caring and student engagement, especially from the perspective of practitioners, is the emphasis on internal states of mind of the students or on dyadic relationships between student and teacher. Some scholars in both literatures, though, are attuned to the way that school culture influences student outcomes. Valenzuela (1999) argues that student disaffection comes from a mismatch between how teachers intend to care about students and how students receive that intended care. Lawson and Lawson (2013) suggest that disengagement is often fostered by "disharmony" between in-school and out-of-school engagement opportunities (p. 462).

In order to better understand the links between caring and engagement as aspects of school climate, this study investigates how the school leaders at Cedarlane Academy intentionally sought to foster a culture of caring and a culture of engagement for both teachers and students. We focus particularly on the ways that the school's status as a charter school both aided and impeded the efforts of school leaders.

METHODS

This study investigates a K–8 charter school located in a large midwestern city in the United States. The student body of 430 is composed almost entirely of first- or 1.5-generation immigrants, mostly from East Africa. The school utilizes the International Baccalaureate (IB) curriculum, which emphasizes the connections between student identity and the world through intercultural understanding and respect. Since its opening in 2008, the school has been considered academically successful based on student achievement scores, a fact currently underscored by its large waiting list of over 1,000 students. The average attendance rate is about 96–98 percent, and a majority of students have attended this school since their kindergarten year.

The case study includes semi-structured interviews of teachers and administrators, participant observation, and an interview method based on photo-elicitation for students. As Merriam (1998) notes, a "case study offers a means of investigating complex social units consisting of multiple variables of potential importance in understanding the phenomenon" (p. 32). In analyzing data, we followed Kvale and Brinkman's (2009) recommendation that interviews, to the extent possible, are self-contained stories that are interpreted within the context of the interview. All interviews were digitally recorded and transcribed, and research conclusions based on respondent answers are cross-checked with respondents to ensure fidelity of meaning.

Researchers visited the school several times over six months to observe classroom instruction, board meetings, teacher conferences, and daily routines of the school. During the several site visits, researchers interviewed 12 teachers across different grade levels and subject areas, 20 students from fifth through eighth grade, and 2 administrators (director and assistant director). Each teacher interview took about 40–60 minutes, focusing on teachers' perceptions of caring and student engagement within the school. The interviews with administrators centered on their leadership effort to manage the school, support school staff as well as students, and create school culture.

For student interviews, we utilized a photo-elicitation research design. Scholars have found that photo-elicitation is a useful tool to understand student perspective and hear their voices, as photography provides a basis for students to share their experience (Clark, 1999; Harper, 2002). Using a photo-elicitation research protocol aligns well with our primary interests in organizational aspects of caring and engagement. The photographs reveal how students perceive the school as a "space" or "place," and thus bring into sharp relief their understanding of the complex social patterns within the school building.

This social pattern not only includes students' personal interactions with their peers and teachers, but also their interactions with other institutional elements like curriculum, structures, and culture. We asked students to take pictures of places in which they "fit in," and the places in which they do not "fit in." Once they brought in the photographs, researchers asked what made them choose these particular places to understand how students perceive the school space in terms of caring and engagement.

As Maxwell (2012) suggests, researcher positionality—"the fact that the researcher is part of the world that he or she studies"—is a "powerful and inescapable influence" (p. 109). Each of the coauthors of this paper is a former high school teacher, and so brought experiences from that professional viewpoint into this research. Two of the authors are white men who taught in U.S. schools, and the third author is a Korean woman whose teaching experience was in a Korean school. Each author is motivated not only by a desire to understand life in schools, but also to help schools function more effectively.

RESULTS

In this section we present, in turn, broad themes from our interviews with school leaders, teachers, and students at Cedarlane Academy. In this section and the discussion that follows, we attend particularly to the way that the charter context shaped outcomes at Cedarlane Academy.

School Leader Interviews

It is important to note that although Cedarlane Academy has both a director (Hanna) and an assistant director (Marissa), both women have been at the school since before it opened. The two women (both of whom are white and middle aged) met while working in the administration of a charter elementary school in a nearby community. Their idea to found Cedarlane Academy emerged from a confluence of ongoing intramural squabbling within the board of directors of the first charter school where they worked, and their exposure to the International Baccalaureate Primary Years Program during school visits to other schools.

For both women, the time spent working together prior to founding their own school based on a shared vision was extremely valuable. As the director noted, "Marissa and I had worked for five years and kind of shared a brain, so we were very philosophically compatible in terms of what we think a school should happen and what should happen in a school." At the same time, both women were also actively building connections in the local community. Consequently, when they opened their own school, Hanna described a "domino effect" of parents choosing to enroll their students in Cedarlane Academy based on their pre-existing relationships with the women.

The process of opening the school took two years of planning (although both Hanna and Marissa remained at their full-time jobs until the nine months immediately prior to the opening of Cedarlane Academy). Though much of this time was spent on securing a building, supplies, and other logistical concerns, a great deal of time was spent envisioning the *climate* of the school. As Marissa put it,

> We spent so much time . . . before we opened the school, [thinking] about what this is going to look like, how it's going to feel, what the teachers are going to say, how they're going to treat their students, how their students will—what kind of a school we wanted to have. A lot of schools will spend a little bit of time on that but then they're so worried about curriculum. Our whole philosophy is that if you don't have the students respecting you and letting you teach, you'll never get the curriculum done anyway. So you have to first tackle that, and have a very respectful atmosphere where you're both communicating, both the teachers and the students have a good relationship, otherwise it doesn't matter what the curriculum is.

From the beginning, school climate was a major focus of the school leaders at Cedarlane Academy. Both Hanna and Marissa emphasized how helpful it was to be able to plan and start a school from the very beginning, in order to more faithfully realize their vision. This planning carried over into staffing the school as well. In the same way that working closely together allowed Hanna and Marissa to develop shared understandings of what makes a school both supportive and rigorous, the ability to interview and select staff allowed them to hire teachers who shared these understandings. As Hanna pointed out:

> You know we're very fortunate because we've hired every person who works at this school, and so you're very fortunate when you start a school, that you get to choose the staff and you can actually interview people and ask them, "What do you believe about kids? What do you believe about student behavior? What do you believe works?" and "What kind of school culture do you want to work in?" So, I think one of the biggest challenges is getting all the adults in the building and on the same page and having the skill set that allows you to do what you want them to do . . . that's the first big challenge. And after that, really, I think everything else pretty much falls into place. I think there needs to be some philosophical compatibility.

The ability to hand-select an entire staff afforded the school leaders at Cedarlane Academy an important advantage in implementing their vision by allowing them to choose teachers who strongly believed in the potential of all students to learn. This is a benefit that is rarely available to school leaders at traditional public schools, or even to charter school leaders who inherit rather than found a new school.

The process of hiring and socializing teachers is ongoing at Cedarlane Academy. Charter schools regularly experience a higher rate of teacher turnover then public district schools (Stuit & Smith, 2010). Hanna and Marissa reported that staff turnover was lower at Cedarlane Academy than at other charter schools where they had worked, but higher than at *district* schools where they previously worked.

During professional development before the school year, new staff members attend off-site cultural training on working with recent North African immigrant students, and are trained in the school's Envoy nonverbal behavior management system. Hanna suggested that hiring new staff often takes two attempts (two years) to find a staff member who can meet Cedarlane Academy's expectations for student success.

Although developing a vision of positive school climate and hiring a staff that could help them realize that vision were important stepping stones to success, school leaders at Cedarlane Academy took three additional steps to create a culture of caring and engagement at the school. First, they adopted a strategy of active supervision. Hanna suggested that teachers who have poorly or incompletely planned lessons are not being respectful of students' time in school. Consequently, they seek to support teachers who "need some help or need resources" while also "cautioning" teachers who are consistently underprepared for lessons. In short, both Hanna and Marissa see helping teachers improve their classroom practice as the most important component of their job.

Second, and closely related, teachers are expected to engage in frequent constructive criticism of one another in order to become better educators. Cedarlane Academy does not engage in traditional professional learning communities. Instead, teachers have 80 minutes of daily coplanning time with their grade-level peers. Twice each quarter, the entire staff comes together in a day-long planning session to present and critique one another's next unit plans, with the intention of bolstering student learning. Hanna and Marissa regularly model this constructive criticism to help ensure that the staff feels supported (and not rebuked). As Hanna states,

> That's something we worked really hard on . . . every once in a while we've had a new teacher who isn't a team player, and the other teachers and the administration would say, "That's not how we operate here, we constructively and positively help each other become better educators. We're not competing, we're not showing off, we're not playing devil's advocates, we're not doing any of those types of things. We're sincere and positive in terms of how we work together." And that's a leadership challenge, to do that.

This way of coplanning reinforces both the high expectations and high support at Cedarlane Academy.

Finally, the school leaders at Cedarlane Academy are acutely aware of the potential for cultural "mismatches" between students and staff. They have actively sought to educate themselves and the teaching staff about the experiences of their students, and have taken a number of commonsense steps to account for student needs. These include constructing the school calendar so that it accounts for the Muslim holidays that Cedarlane Academy's students celebrate, as well as the Christian holidays celebrated by much of the staff, and ensuring that teachers do not schedule field trips for Friday (the Muslim holy day) so that students do not have to choose between a field trip and going to the mosque with their families.

Another way in which school leaders seek to be culturally responsive is by responding to parent concerns and requests with as much flexibility as possible. Hanna and Marissa encourage teachers to change assignments and guidelines based on parents' input.

The sections below detail themes from interviews with students and teachers. One major finding of this study is that the modeling and expectations from the school leaders at Cedarlane Academy impact the way that teachers interact with one another *and* with students.

Teacher Interviews

Several themes emerged from the teacher interviews at Cedarlane Academy. First, every teacher interviewed reported a high degree of caring and mutual support from other staff members. One teacher stated,

> And then even if staff members are sick but they're here, other staff members are like, you can take care of [being sick]. And I really feel like everyone is so caring here, like honestly, I've never been in another school where . . . I've been in other schools where teachers . . . collaborate [on one unit] and they'll talk, but outside of that there is really nothing and I feel like a lot of people just kind of work within that, and at this school it's like, I can go up to the kindergarten teachers, I can go up to first, second grade and you know, see what they're doing, talk, talk about different management strategies, and there is so much collaboration here; it's really great.

The sense among teachers of genuine regard for one another, as well as a willingness to engage high levels of professional collaboration, was very strong. In part, this collaboration is a by-product of the school's International Baccalaureate curriculum. As one teacher noted,

> Well, I think that [because] we're an international baccalaureate school . . . [when we are thinking about] our Units of Inquiry and planning for those and collaborating and coming up with things that we think will be topics not only necessarily to teach, but also that will be highly engaging topics that would be exciting for the kids to learn about, and will spark interest and inquiry and make them want to learn more about them. So I think that, just that our curriculum in general is a high-student-interest type of curriculum.

In important ways, the choice of curriculum shapes interaction among teachers by necessitating collaboration. At the same time, the warm and supportive tone of that collaboration comes, in large part, from school administrators. The administration sets a tone of high support for teachers in terms of financial help for classroom projects, and giving teachers choices about instruction. As one teacher noted, "I think giving teachers choice . . . I don't think I've ever gone to Hanna and Marissa and said, 'I wanted to do this,' and their response was 'No.' It's always, 'Well, how could we make that happen?' You know, 'What do you need from us?'"

Although the school leaders expressed that charter school finances occasionally constrained them, they both talked about the importance of empowering teachers to achieve their curricular goals. There was consensus among teachers that this culture of collegiality, collaboration, and personal and professional support make Cedarlane Academy a caring place to work. School leaders were able to set an example of support (along with high expectations), and this example also characterized relations between teachers.

Teachers mostly thought about caring for their students in two ways. First, caring involved knowing what was going on with students, particularly knowing what was happening out of school and in students' home lives. Second, caring for students involved a notion of fairness. As one teacher put it,

> I think what the students see as caring, they know the expectation, and they also will see that I'm consistent with everyone. And I think when you're consistent with everybody, they feel that same, like, you know, I'm not going to favor somebody else. I'm not going to treat someone differently, you know. If you do a certain action, the consequence, or the outcome is the exact same for everybody, regardless, if you are consistent, direction-follower . . . the outcome is the same.

This conceptualization of caring as a combination of interest and consistent, fair use of teacher power was prevalent among teachers.

Teachers also suggested that the Units of Inquiry associated with the IB curriculum were useful for activating empathy and engagement among students precisely because the school contained diverse student perspectives. As one teacher stated,

> I think it goes back to the fact that . . . it's such a global perspective here. And really, administration is always pushing the global perspective here too, which I think is just amazing because this year I'm about to teach, I can't remember right now if its seventh or eighth grade, but it's civil wars. And we really focused on the American civil war for quite some time and over the past several years its morphed into looking at other civil wars internationally, and that's actually what their research project is going to be, to research a civil war and then basically give a report card on those leaders, so it's going to be really interesting to see what they come up with.

Another teacher identified a similar effect:

> The strengths of the school, the fact that it's International Baccalaureate, you get that global perspective. I really wish in middle school or high school I went to a school that had that because, I have a pretty empathetic perspective when I'm teaching, it's the way that I think. You're putting yourself in other people's shoes daily and it's what empathy is. I feel like the kids who are starting to pick that up, you can see it in the school. You can see that some of the students truly care for one another. They will be helping each other out, or especially in the eighth grade, they've known each other for years and years now, and just the way they're able to talk to one another even if they're upset or angry.

This teacher is identifying the intentional aspects of empathy present in the global orientation of the curriculum, as well as the sense of continuity among students, as central to student engagement. In popular shorthand, the students at Cedarlane Academy might be referred to as "disadvantaged" or "at risk," but the school leaders and staff have leveraged the diverse student experiences at the school in ways that foster both empathy and engagement. Particularly over time, student's knowledge and experiences with one another become an important part of learning.

Student Interviews

Photo-elicitation was an effective means to garner student opinions about the school environment. Students were prompted to take pictures of locations in the school building where they felt that they "fit in" or "do not fit in." In interviews, students were prompted with the photograph and asked why they elected to take a photo of that particular place or aspect of the school. The student's explanation of the meaning they ascribed to various spaces within the school was integral in helping the researchers to understand how students experience the school environment and, more importantly, how the institutional aspects of the school environment facilitate students' social and emotional connections to the school.

Out of the total of 110 pictures, 92 (84%) were taken of places where students felt that they "fit in," and the balance (18 pictures, 16%) were of places where students felt that they "did not fit in." In being prompted to take pictures, students were not steered toward any particular balance of belonging versus not belonging. The distribution of belonging to not belonging is thus simply a product of student choices. In general, students seemed to have a quite positive view of the school as a caring environment.

Evidently, caring is present from the time students enter school. As one student noted,

> I chose the school entry because I think—because every morning there is people there to greet you. It's not like any other school where you just walk in by yourself, that will, like, greet you and ask you how you are. I think the school—also the symbol for how the school's also a very caring school, and they care how much you learn.

Throughout the interviews, it became clear that students' sense of being cared for was multifaceted. Students' personal relationships with teachers were important, but so too were students' perceptions of teachers' attitudes toward their entire class. Students had a sense for teachers caring about them as individuals, but their view of teaching was also shaped by how the teacher acted toward peers (even peers who were not close friends). The actions of school leaders in student discipline also contributed to students' sense of belonging to the school.

In particular, students described the importance of teachers' efforts to include the entire class in activities, and of not censuring students who answered questions incorrectly. Students, like teachers, felt that equitable distribution of support among the group was important. One fifth-grade student described her gym class: "'Cause I feel that the gym is a very welcoming place and like, if you, like, don't know how to do one thing, they don't, like, kick you out of the group, they teach you as a whole and it's not, like, they don't cancel you out just 'cause you can't do one simple thing. They help everybody."

Peer relationships were also central to student feelings of belonging. Students repeatedly identified their gym class and homeroom as places they belong because they are places where students can socialize with their friends. In addition to peer relationships, some students actually emphasized particular elements of their classroom, such as the classroom library, grammar boards, or math calendar. For these students, these particular aspects of the classroom aligned with particular academic interests. Inviting classroom spaces contributed in important ways to student engagement and sense of belonging.

Student perception of the dispositions of school leaders also provided an interesting insight into students' sense of belonging at school. Eight students took pictures of the school's administrative offices. Of these, five pictures were described by students as places they didn't feel like they "fit in." These students associated the administrative offices as places that made them "nervous" or places to send students who "got in trouble."

On the other hand, three students described the dean's office as a place where they did feel like they "fit in." Each of these students described the dean as a person who listened to and validated their thoughts, and a person whom they trusted to be fair. Importantly, the students who had a positive association with the dean's office were the students who most frequently actually got into trouble at school. One student noted:

> This is the picture of Mr. Muhammad's [dean's] office and I like it because he does one-on-one conversation and he allows us to just talk. Whatever you say is, kind of stays with us, and he really knows us. He just tells us what to do and what not to do in conversations and he, kind of, puts people together. Just kind of, put our differences aside so we can focus on our academics, I really like that.

Mr. Muhammad is the only member of the school administration that comes from the same ethnic background as the students at the school. The school leadership at Cedarlane Academy purposefully chose Arabic as the school's foreign language as a reflection of the student body. This choice of foreign language, in student's eyes, contributed to their sense of belonging to the school. As one student noted, "Arabic is my language."

Students who are practicing Muslims (which is to say, the majority) are allowed to observe *salah* during class time. One student summarized the school environment thus:

> This place is really open and it's kind of caring because, like, through the front doors you see Miss J and Miss D and they always have a smile on their faces, and they're, like, it's a very welcome place. It feels like family basically, and it's not that kind of family where you just argue but it's where you—like, you know—the teachers really know you and they take time to understand who you are because they know who you are. . . . It's the bond that they create during the first moment that I walk in, really like that.

Perhaps the most striking theme that emerged throughout student photographs and interviews was the sense of continuity that students felt at Cedarlane Academy. A significant portion of students took pictures of either their kindergarten or early elementary classrooms, and described them as places where they felt that they "fit in." Many students described how they felt a sense of belonging at the school because they had memories of multiple teachers and classrooms across multiple years. One important way that the school leaders at Cedarlane Academy have created a culture of caring for students is simply by ensuring a high degree of stability in the student body, and a strong sense of familiarity with the school that grows over time.

IMPLICATIONS FOR PRACTICE

The original purpose of this case study was to explore the relationship between educational caring and student engagement, particularly (1) the ways that caring and engagement are fostered at a school-wide level, and not merely between individuals; and (2) in a school setting that scholars have identified as potentially problematic due to significant cultural differences between school staff and students. In this section, we identify some important implications for practicing charter school leaders that emerged from the case of Cedarlane Academy.

First, teachers clearly identified the diverse student perspectives at Cedarlane Academy as an asset that can pay educational dividends. The diversity of student experiences at the school allows teachers to design highly engaging Units of Inquiry, whereby students can learn about their classmates and global events. Teachers described this curriculum as not only highly engaging, but also as productive in terms of empathy and mutual regard. Although the IB curriculum at the school was helpful to facilitate this at Cedarlane Academy, there is no a priori reason that any school could not plan units to help students learn about one another in empathy-producing ways.

The high proportion of immigrants at Cedarlane Academy made an international focus particularly appropriate, but a curriculum focused on building understanding in more local ways could be similarly effective. The differences among students, and between students and teachers, are thus used to promote and reinforce notions of global citizenship at Cedarlane Academy. This narrative stands in stark contrast to the process of alienation and cultural divestment described by Valenzuela (1999).

The school leaders at Cedarlane Academy supported this practice by purposefully making curricular choices that highlight students' background and interests (e.g., language instruction in Arabic), while also supporting teachers' experimentation and *expecting* teachers to highlight student life experiences in their curriculum planning. Although the composition of the student body at Cedarlane Academy lends itself to emphasizing notions of global citizenship, charter school leaders in any setting can leverage their own particular student experiences in ways that enhance engagement and sense of belonging.

A second implication for practice relates to students' sense of belonging at Cedarlane Academy. For many students, a sense of belonging at the school was tied up in a sense of continuity with the school community. Students' ability to identify experiences, feelings, and relationships from peers and teachers over the course of six, seven, eight, or even nine years contributes to a sense of embeddedness within the school community. Although students' level of engagement with school ebbs and flows over time, for Cedarlane Academy students the ebbs and flows are tethered to multiple years of impressions and experiences.

This finding is particularly interesting given the demographic and cultural differences between teachers and students. Except for the three Arabic teachers, the rest of staff are mostly white women from middle-class backgrounds who were born in the United States. For many scholars and practitioners, the "demographic divide" between teachers and students has been considered a critical social justice issue in education, because it has the potential to lead to student disengagement from school (Darling-Hammond & Bransford, 2007).

The school leaders at Cedarlane Academy took multiple steps to bridge this divide, but the most important appears to have been sustained positive interactions for students over the course of multiple years of school. Although charter school principals cannot always exercise perfect control over students (or teachers) leaving their schools, this finding underscores the power of stability in increasing students' sense of belonging.

Additionally, Cedarlane Academy is characterized by layers of mutual support. Every teacher interviewed by the researchers described a high level of both personal caring and professional collaboration among the staff. Teachers also experienced a high degree of support from school leaders, and felt empowered by administrators to pursue ambitious instructional goals.

The tone of support between school staff members is similar to the way students described being cared for by teachers. At Cedarlane Academy, this sort of caring is a way-of-being in relation to others; the particular manner of the culture of care at Cedarlane Academy structures interpersonal relations throughout the school.

The implication for charter school principals is that the relationships between school leaders and teachers (and among teachers) will closely mirror the relationship between teachers and students. A high-support and high-expectations environment is modeled by school leaders for teachers. Because charter schools are often not embedded in larger networks, charter school leaders have a greater ability to set the tone of interaction among staff than, for example, principals of schools in large districts have.

Finally, students experience caring and engagement as classroom-level attributes. Although students did speak in interviews about their relationships with teachers, other school staff, and peers, they also spoke often about the way that teachers treated and interacted with their entire class. This student perception of teacher disposition toward groups of their peers offers evidence that students do not think narrowly about caring as interpersonal relations, but make sense of their entire environment as a caring or engaging place. A closely related finding is that student perceptions of caring and engagement appear to involve iterations of reorientation based on environmental factors.

Perceptions of cultural difference and alignment play a role in these reorientations. Students appear to continually assess the extent to which school staff knows them, but also the extent to which the school environment reflects their own identity. Students at Cedarlane Academy are thus not engaged in wholesale assimilation (Ogbu, 1990). Rather, the students negotiate school in terms of their identities and experiences, and renegotiate their identities and outside experiences in terms of school.

School leaders at Cedarlane Academy were engaged in a continuous process of building and reinforcing a culture of care and engagement in school; staff did not merely establish good relationships with students, but critically examined their practices over time as well.

At Cedarlane Academy, educational caring and student engagement are related to students' perceived degree of alignment between the school environment and the students' own identities and experiences. Importantly, this alignment does not occur only in terms of individual relationships, but also at the classroom and organizational level, and across time. The staff at Cedarlane purposefully create curriculum that allows for the recognition and affirmation of diverse student experiences, and seek to cultivate a sense of global citizenship in order to both increase student engagement and produce greater empathy among students. Generally, students as Cedarlane Academy feel a strong sense of belonging to school.

CONCLUSION

As noted above, this study has several broader implications for both school leaders and policy makers. First, the extent to which a school's vision of student citizenship allows student experiences to be shared and reflected at school appears to have important implications for students' sense of belonging, particularly at schools with a high proportion of recent immigrants.

Moreover, caring at Cedarlane Academy was a practice layered throughout the school, not something that teachers and staff did to or for students. The high degree of professional collaboration among staff, and empowerment of teachers by the school administration, were paired with personal regard for one another. These multiple layers of authentic caring appear to mediate interactions among both students and staff in a way that a more instrumental version of caring would not. Finally, continuity appears to matter for students' engagement with school.

It seems clear that the way students experience caring in schools has real implications for the level of student engagement and their sense of belonging. The charter context at Cedarlane Academy allowed school leaders to purposefully build a climate of caring and engagement in several ways. The principal was able to select a teaching staff that shared her belief that all students can learn.

Through a mixture of high support and high expectations for teachers, the leaders empowered teachers to make curricular choices that leveraged student experiences to create both engagement and a sense of caring. Furthermore, by creating a thoughtfully ordered school environment, the school leaders at Cedarlane Academy were able to create a sense of stability that helped students feel more and more connected to school as time passed.

The charter context allowed Cedarlane Academy school leaders to execute their vision with minimal interference from, for example, a district office. To be more specific, the school leaders were able to exercise autonomy in selecting their school staff, plan training for the staff on academic and behavioral expectations for students, and leverage considerable flexibility in continuously tweaking their vision in response to feedback from staff, students, and parents. For example, early in the school's existence, the school leaders changed the school calendar to better align with the observances of both students and staff. In a word, the charter context allowed leaders at Cedarlane Academy to be more *nimble*.

On the other hand, the school leaders did not have access to the institutional support that a district office may have provided. For example, although the school leaders at Cedarlane Academy were invested in providing high-quality training for their staff, the planning and execution of this training fell entirely on Hanna and Marissa; they were not able to leverage the expertise that a district might have. Moreover, although the school has maintained excellent financial health, the financial planning portions of school leadership place significant demands on Hanna and Marissa's time.

In the case of Cedarlane Academy, these challenges have been met and surmounted; the advantages outweigh the disadvantages. However, other charter schools have not been as successful. More study is needed to better understand why some charter school principals are so effective at achieving their educational visions, while others are less so.

REFERENCES

Ancess, J. (2000). The reciprocal influence of teacher learning, teaching practice, school restructuring, and student learning outcomes. *Teachers College Record, 102*(3), 590–619.

Antrop-González, R., & De Jesús, A. (2006). Toward a theory of critical care in urban small school reform: Examining structures and pedagogies of caring in two Latino community-based schools. *International Journal of Qualitative Studies in Education, 19*(4), 409–433. http://dx.doi.org/10.1080/09518390600773148

Bartlett, L., & García, O. (2011). *Additive schooling in subtractive times: Dominican immigrant youth in the heights*. Nashville, TN: Vanderbilt University Press.

Battistich, V., Solomon, D., Kim, D.-I., Watson, M., & Schaps, E. (1995). Schools as communities, poverty levels of student populations, and students' attitudes, motives, and performance: A multilevel analysis. *American Educational Research Journal, 32*(3), 627–658.

Battistich, V., Solomon, D., Watson, M., & Schaps, E. (1997). Caring school communities. *Educational Psychologist, 32*(3), 137–151. http://dx.doi.org/10.1207/s15326985ep3203_1

Clark, C. D. (1999). The autodriven interview: A photographic viewfinder into children's experience. *Visual Studies, 14*(1), 39–50.

Darling-Hammond, L., & Bransford, J. (2007). *Preparing teachers for a changing world: What teachers should learn and be able to do*. San Francisco: John Wiley & Sons.

Darling-Hammond, L., & Sclan, E. M. (1996). Who teaches and why: Dilemmas of building a profession for twenty-first century schools. In J. Sikula (Ed.), *Handbook of research on teacher education* (vol. 2, pp. 67–101). New York: Simon & Schuster.

Duncan-Andrade, J. (2007). Urban youth and the counter-narration of inequality. *Transforming Anthropology, 15*(1), 26–37.

Duncan-Andrade, J. (2009). Note to educators: Hope required when growing roses in concrete. *Harvard Educational Review, 79*(2), 181–194.

Durlak, J. A., Weissberg, R. P., & Pachan, M. (2010). A meta-analysis of after-school programs that seek to promote personal and social skills in children and adolescents. *American Journal of Community Psychology, 45*(3–4), 294–309.

Epstein, J. L. (2001). *School, family, and community partnerships: Preparing educators and improving schools*. Boulder, CO: Westview Press.

Hargreaves, A., Earl, L., & Ryan, J. (1996). *Schooling for change: reinventing schools for early adolescents*. London: Falmer.

Harper, D. (2002). Talking about pictures: A case for photo elicitation. *Visual Studies, 17*(1), 13–26.

Hoffman, D. M. (2009). Reflecting on social emotional learning: A critical perspective on trends in the United States. *Review of Educational Research, 79*(2), 533–556.

Kvale, S., & Brinkman, S. (2009). *Interviews: Learning the craft of qualitative interviewing*. London: Sage.

Lawson, M. A., & Lawson, H. A. (2013). New conceptual frameworks for student engagement: Research, policy, and practice. *Review of Educational Research, 83*(3), 432–479.

Lee, V. E., & Smith, J. B. (1999). Social support and achievement for young adolescents in Chicago: The role of school academic press. *American Educational Research Journal, 36*(4), 907–945.

Marks, H. M. (2000). Student engagement in instructional activity: Patterns in the elementary, middle, and high school years. *American Educational Research Journal, 37*(1), 153–184.

Maxwell, J. A. (2012). *Qualitative research design: An interactive approach.* Los Angeles: Sage.

McKamey, C. (2011). Restorying "caring" in education: Students' narratives of caring *for* and *about. Narrative Works, 1*(1). Retrieved from https://journals.lib.unb.ca/index.php/NW/article/view/18475/19976

Merriam, S. B. (1998). *Qualitative research and case study applications in education.* San Francisco: Jossey-Bass.

Noddings, N. (1992). *The challenge to care in schools* (2nd ed.). New York: Teachers College Press.

Noddings, N. (2005). Identifying and responding to needs in education. *Cambridge Journal of Education, 35*(2), 147–159.

Noddings, N. (2006). Educational leaders as caring teachers. *School Leadership & Management, 26*(4), 339–345. http://dx.doi.org/10.1080/13632430600886848

Noddings, N. (2013). *Caring: A relational approach to ethics and moral education.* Berkeley: University of California Press.

Ogbu, J. U. (1990). Minority education in comparative perspective. *Journal of Negro Education, 59*(1), 45–57.

Reschly, A. L., & Christenson, S. L. (2012). Jingle, jangle, and conceptual haziness: Evolution and future directions of the engagement construct. In S. L. Christenson, A. L. Reschly, & C. Wylie (Eds.), *Handbook of research on student engagement* (pp. 3–19). New York: Springer.

Riley, K. (2013a). *Leadership of place: Stories from schools in the US, UK and South Africa.* London: Bloomsbury Academic.

Riley, K. A. (2013b). Walking the leadership tightrope: Building community cohesiveness and social capital in schools in highly disadvantaged urban communities. *British Educational Research Journal, 39*(2), 266–286.

Rolón-Dow, R. (2005). Critical care: A color (full) analysis of care narratives in the schooling experiences of Puerto Rican girls. *American Educational Research Journal, 42*(1), 77–111.

Stuit, D., & Smith, T. M. (2010). *Teacher turnover in charter schools.* Nashville, TN: National Center on School Choice, Vanderbilt University (NJ1).

Thompson, A. (1998). Not the Color Purple: Black feminist lessons for educational caring. *Harvard Educational Review, 68*(4), 522–555. http://dx.doi.org/10.17763/haer.68.4.nm436v83214n5016

Tronto, J. C. (2010). Creating caring institutions: Politics, plurality, and purpose. *Ethics and Social Welfare, 4*(2), 158–171.

Valenzuela, A. (1999). *Subtractive schooling: Issues of caring in education of US-Mexican youth.* Albany: State University of New York Press.

Wentzel, K. R. (1997). Student motivation in middle school: The role of perceived pedagogical caring. *Journal of Educational Psychology, 89*(3), 411.

Chapter Four

Principal Change in an Existing Charter School

What Happens to Mission, Vision, and Culture?

Dana L. Bickmore

Kids Korner Charter School (all names are pseudonyms) is one of the oldest charters in a southern state. This case study began at the commencement of Kids Korner's twelfth year operating as a single-choice charter elementary school.

One of the few schools in the state chartered under the local school district, Kids Korner focused on serving at-risk students in a nurturing environment. As stated in the charter and subsequent reauthorization documents,

> The mission of Kids Korner Elementary School is to serve as a model for implementation of an innovative, flexible educational program, which targets at-risk students. . . . It is in the best interest of these at-risk students that they are given the opportunity for continued success within this small, nurturing environment. . . . The philosophy of Kids Korner is to acknowledge the challenges faced by our students and their families and to seek help and support for these families.

According to teachers and local school district administrators, Kids Korner held true to this mission since its inception; at least 90 percent of the students received free and reduced lunch, and at least 95 percent of the students were African American.

The school institutionalized structures and practices outlined in the original charter that were designed to achieve a nurturing environment and school culture. The school had remained small, with approximately 240 students in kindergarten through fifth grade. Classes were limited to no more than 20 students, with one paraprofessional assigned to each teacher. Parent communication was regularly scheduled through formal and informal conferences and social events, such as "friendship suppers." The school had also institutionalized a voluntary extended day program for which teachers and local agencies provided various enrichment activities to students and families who wished to participate.

The nurturing environment and culture also extended to the instructional staff, where there was little teacher turnover; several of the founding staff, including the principal, remained at the school through the 12 years of operation. In year 13, however, the founding principal retired, and Kids Korner changed radically. The purpose of this single case study was to examine how principal change at this established charter school affected mission, vision and, ultimately, school culture.

THE DILEMMA OF CULTURAL DEVELOPMENT, CONTINUITY, AND ADAPTABILITY

Whether a single school such as Kids Korner, or a set of schools managed by nonprofit or for-profit entities, charter schools are organizations. There is a natural tension in any organization, the need for flexibility and autonomy and, at the same time, the need for stability. Flexibility and autonomy provide organizations the ability to innovate and adapt to new situations. At the same time, organizations need stability in their structures, norms, values, and beliefs to avoid chaos and to promote survival. As Schein (2010) suggested, "Organizations face two archetypical problems: (1) survival in and adaptation to the external environment, and (2) integration of the internal processes to ensure the capacity to continue to survive and adapt" (p. 73). Balancing both change and stability is an ongoing struggle in most organizations.

According to Schein (2010), the purpose of an organization's culture is to balance the two competing tensions of change and stability. Functioning cultures are able to balance both adaptation/change and internal integrity. Cultures provide both the necessary stability for goal attainment, and the flexibility to grow and innovate. Organizational cultures become dysfunctional when they no longer help the organization adapt, or the culture leads to instability and chaos. Dysfunctional cultures can lead to the complete destruction of the organization.

Cultures form through organizational members sharing a concept of purpose (mission), a view of an ideal future for the school (vision), and agreed-upon goals, norms, values, and beliefs (Deal & Peterson, 2010; Gruenert & Whitaker, 2015). The development of culture in charter schools may be different from that of traditional public schools because of external expectations and policies, such as the greater autonomy given charters in exchange for performance and the need to recruit students.

Charter schools were born and continue to be touted as organizations of innovation (Lubienski & Weitzel, 2010). State policies provide charter schools with autonomy regarding rules and regulations required of traditional public schools, to encourage change and innovation. State authorization policies frequently require founders to outline a unique purpose for the school (mission), with a compelling vision that often designates school structures and practices. The charter, in essence, is meant to outline innovation, but in a single moment in time. As charter schools age, the original mission, vision, goals, and processes outlined may not allow for adaptability.

LEADERSHIP AND CULTURAL DEVELOPMENT AND ADAPTION

The charter and the intent of the founders are guideposts for culture building; however, people within the organization actually create the culture as they interact with each other to solve problems (Deal & Peterson, 2010; Schein, 2010). No one person can dictate what the organizational culture will be. However, to achieve the mission, vision, and goals outlined through the charter, school members must embrace these concepts and incorporate them in how they operate within the school. These building blocks of culture are just that—ingredients of a potential school culture.

Although the school culture cannot be dictated, leadership plays a key role in supporting its development. Deal and Peterson (1999) suggest that "school leaders can nudge the process along through their actions, conversations, decision, and public pronouncements" (p. 85). Research confirms the importance of leadership that fosters common purpose (mission), a view of an ideal future for the school (vision), and shared norms and goals in developing a culture of student success (Edmonds, 1979; Purkey & Smith, 1982; Sammons, 1995).

Current organizational theories that focus on leadership and culture outline types of leadership interactions between the leader and those led, which may contribute to building, maintaining, and changing culture (Alvesson, 2011; Bolman & Deal, 2013; Northouse, 2013). Bass and Avolio (1993, 1994) proposed a continuum of how leaders interact with followers. On one end of the continuum, leaders have limited interaction, with followers taking a laissez-faire leadership role.

Moving to the middle of the continuum, leaders take on transactional interactions, in that they "exchange things of value with subordinates to advance their own and their subordinates' agenda" (Northouse, 2013, p. 195). Leaders lay out specific tasks and provide rewards for completing the tasks. Leaders use corrective actions, such as negative feedback, reproof, or disciplinary action, when performance deviates from the leader's expectations.

Bass and Avolio (1993) suggest that transformational leadership, at the opposite end of the continuum from laissez-faire leadership, is a more effective interaction process between leader and follower in developing a culture that accomplishes individual and organizational goals. Transformational leadership is characterized by leaders acting as role models, inspiring follower motivation through collaboration, supporting innovation, and focusing on follower needs. Research specific to educational leadership suggests increased principal engagement in transformational leadership practices improves student outcomes, because teachers are more likely to focus on agreed-upon norms and values related to school mission, vision, and goals—the building blocks of school culture (Leithwood & Jantzi, 1990, 2000).

How leaders interact with followers is important, but what they do in relation to organizational structures and actions are also important. Bass and Avolio (1993) state:

> Leaders create mechanisms for cultural development and the reinforcement of norms and behaviors expressed within the boundaries of the culture. Cultural norms arise and change because of what leaders focus their attention on, how they react to crises, the behaviors they role model, and whom they attract to their organizations. The characteristics and qualities of an organization's culture are taught by its leadership and eventually adopted by its followers. (p. 113)

In his foundational book on organizational cultures, Schein (2010) outlined primary and secondary mechanisms by which leaders embed and reinforce culture (table 4.1).

Gruenert and Whitaker (2015) specifically examined school culture development and suggested that there are six types of cultures that are progressively more effective for student outcomes, ranging from toxic, to fragmented, balkanized, contrived collegial, comfortable collaborative, and collaborative.

Once a school culture has solidified, whether effective or not, it becomes difficult to change (Gruenert & Whitaker, 2015). Schein (2010) noted, "Embedding new assumptions in a mature organization is much more difficult than in a young and growing organization because all of the organization structures and processes have to be rethought and, perhaps, rebuilt" (p. 294). According to Schein (2010), organizations' cultures move through three stages of maturity based on their growth, age, stability, and adaption to the external environment. These three stages are founding and early growth, midlife, and maturity and potential decline.

Table 4.1. Primary and Secondary Mechanisms to Embed and Reinforce Culture

Primary Embedded Mechanisms	Secondary Articulation and Reinforcement Mechanisms
What leaders pay attention to, measure, and control on a regular basis	Organizational design and structure
How leaders react to critical incidents and organizational crises	Organizational systems and procedures
How leaders allocate resources	Rites and rituals of the organization
Deliberate role modeling, teaching, and coaching	Design of physical space, facades, and buildings
How leaders allocate rewards and status	Stories about important events and people
How leaders recruit, select, promote, and excommunicate	Formal statements of organizational philosophy, creeds, and charters

Source: Schein, 2010, p. 236.

Leaders influence cultural change, depending on the stage of the organization. In the founding and early growth stage, culture is mainly dependent on the founders and their assumptions. The initial principal in a new charter school may be one of the founders, or may be hired by those who developed and were passionate about the mission, vision, and idealized culture set out in the charter (Merseth, 2009). The first principal is highly likely to engage in developing the culture set by the founders, using Schein's embedding and reinforcing mechanisms.

According to Schein (2010), "Organizational midlife can be defined structurally as the stage at which founder owners have relinquished the control of the organization to promoted or appointed general managers" (p. 280). In the organizational maturity and potential decline stage, organizational assumptions, espoused values, ideals, and beliefs become solidified. If the internal and external environment stays stable, these strongly held assumptions, processes, and procedures within the organization can be an advantage, providing stability for the organization to operate smoothly and efficiently. However, if the environment changes and the organizational culture does not evolve, the stability limits adaptation, and leads to declining organizational effectiveness.

All of the cultural embedding mechanisms that support development of a culture may be employed to change a midlife or mature culture. Schein (2010) suggested that additional intentional mechanisms might also be needed to change midlife and mature cultures. At midlife, strategically promoting individuals from one of the organization's subcultures can shift the culture of the organization in incremental ways. Introducing a technology that changes processes in the organization is another method of culture change. The third mechanism used by leaders for change comes when the governing board brings in a new leader from outside the organization. This mechanism often leads to incremental cultural change, unless the new leader is strategic about maintaining the existing culture.

Board or public perceptions that an organization is dysfunctional often lead to the most radical change mechanism—turnaround efforts. In this process, a leader is hired to intentionally reorganize and change culture. Through turnaround, mature cultures may experience complete destruction and rebirth. This occurs through replacing not only the leader, but also large numbers of personnel in order to create the new culture.

The charter movement is now in its third decade, and little research has examined how stable, mature charter schools have experienced the tension of cultural changes as a result of leadership change. Limited research suggests changes in principal leadership in traditional schools may impact school culture (Hall & George, 1999). However, one of the cornerstones of charter schooling is the autonomy given the school leader (Wohlstetter, Smith, & Farrell, 2013). How might the greater principal autonomy provided to charter school principals affect school culture when the founding principal leaves? How did changing the principal at Kids Korner affect the mission, vision, and ultimately the culture of the school, outlined by the charter and implemented by the founding principal?

STUDY BACKGROUND

This single case study was part of a larger three-year comparative case study (Yin, 2012) of charter school principal leadership in a southern state. In the original study, Kids Korner was selected both for convenience and for specific purposes (Collins, Onwuegbuzie, & Jiao, 2007). Kids Korner was one of 10 charter school asking for help and support from a local university. Kids Korner was purposely selected for the original study because it represented several unique characteristics: it was a long running charter school, it was authorized by the local school district, the principal was in his first year as the study began, and the school was opening a middle school (grades 6–8) in the first year of the study.

Kids Korner became of particular interest as a separate case study because of the ways in which the new principal's leadership unfolded over the three years. The school became a prime case for addressing the question supporting this research: how does principal change at an established charter school affected mission, vision and, ultimately, school culture?

Data Sources and Analysis

Data sources included in-depth, semi-structured principal and teacher interviews, and field notes of observations, artifacts, and documents, including the charter application. The primary data sources were 26 principal and teacher semi-structured interviews, lasting from 10 to 90 minutes. The principal, Mr. Clark, was interviewed at least twice a year. Initially, three teachers were randomly selected to participate and be interviewed twice a year over the three years. However, due to teacher turnover, each year new teachers were purposefully selected for interviewing. Additionally, the designated instructional coach was interviewed each year.

In total, there were 11 interviews with principals and 15 with teachers and instructional coaches (table 4.2). Although interview questions varied by year and participant group in the larger study, in each interview, all participants were asked, "What were the principal's priorities?" and "Describe the climate and culture of the school."

With the exception of the original charter to the state, the collected artifacts, observations, and documents were used to confirm interview data. The actual charter to the state provided an outline of the mission, vision, and structures promoted by the founders to build culture. Artifacts included regular downloads of the school's web page; student recruiting materials; instructional and curriculum materials collected by the principal; pictures of decorations and inspirational materials, such as those posted on walls and awards given to children; and newsletters to parents.

Observations included shadowing the principal for at least half of the day each year; parent meetings; classroom observations; and student activities

Table 4.2. Participants

Participant	Role	Years at School Prior to Study	Years at School During Study	Times Interviewed
Clark	Principal	0	3	11
Wiley	Teacher	6	1	2
Soto	Teacher	0	1	2
Davis	Instructional coach	3	2	3
Moyer	Teacher	12 (founding)	1	2
Levy	Teacher	0		2
Johnson	Instructional coach	0	1	2
Lawrence	Teacher	0	1	1

before, during, and after school. Beyond the charter application, documents included faculty lists and Department of Education charter information, such as school and district demographics and public information about teacher certification.

In the original study, the data was first coded in an eclectic manner (Saldaña, 2013), applying different types of codes to data related to the principals' leadership dispositions, knowledge, skills, and practices. These first-level codes were used when Kids Korner became a single embedded case (Stake, 2006). Codes were then consolidated into categories, and categories were analyzed in relation to Schein's (2010) stated mechanisms that leaders use to embed and shape culture. Additionally, since leaders shape culture over time (Gruenert & Whitaker, 2015), a longitudinal coding scheme (Saldaña, 2013) was applied to compare categories with Schein's culture-shaping mechanisms each year. This resulted in themes representing how the change in principal affected school culture. These comparisons resulted in three themes that represented culture development over time.

The processes of credibility, transferability, dependability, and conformability were employed to address and provide confidence in the research. The author and one other researcher initially coded transcripts and documents from the first year together, line by line and side by side (Stake, 2006). Additionally, the author employed extensive analytic memos, prolonged engagement with the case (Creswell, 2013), multiple sources of evidence (Yin, 2009), multiple researchers in data analysis (Stake, 2006), and checks with participants to affirm the facts of the case (Patton, 2002; Yin, 2009).

School and Principal Background

The Kids Korner board hired the founding principal as the charter application was developed; the principal retired from the school after 12 years at the helm. The Kids Korner board then hired Mr. Clark to replace the founding principal. Clark held two degrees, one in economics and the other in African studies. After working for a consulting firm for three years, Clark moved to the state from New York as a Teach for America (TFA) teacher and obtained alternate teacher certification after his second year of teaching. Clark taught middle school mathematics for two years in a traditional public school with a high percentage of minority students and students receiving free and reduced lunch.

In his third year in education, Clark took on a teacher/administrator position at a district-sponsored autonomous high school serving at-risk students. He also worked part time and then full time for one year for the State Department of Education (SDOE) to prepare groups of individuals who wanted to apply and open charter schools. Unlike his predecessor, Clark had no principal experience and did not have principal certification; he came to the principalship with three years of teaching experience and one year at the SDOE.

During the first year of the study, the teaching staff at Kids Korner was experienced and stable. All but six of the sixteen teachers, one instructional coach, and eight teaching assistants had been at the school more than two years. Of the six new instructional staff, four were hired to open the new middle school. The average experience in the classroom was six years. Three instructional personnel, two teachers, and one teaching assistant had been at the school since it opened. Three of the four teaching staff interviewed the first year had been at the school for three or more years, with one teacher being a founding teacher and one new to the school (see table 4.2).

As the study began, Kids Korner had grown to 277 students with the addition of a middle school of 40 students. For the first two years of the study, the school was labeled a two-star school (out of five stars), based primarily on the state-mandated standardized test. The school had consistently been a two-star school, which kept it from threats of closure by state accountability standards, as one-star schools were subject to possible nonrenewal. The state test and accountability requirements changed in the third year, making it difficult to compare the school's third-year performance with the first two years. The rating system moved from a star system to a letter grade, which put the school at a C average.

Kids Korner was a single school, with a nonprofit corporation governing only this school. One member of the founding board remained on the board when Clark was hired. The school board did not use a charter management organization, and contracted services directly as needed. The school was eligible for and had been authorized by the district for some district services. Clark reported directly to the board, had full autonomy in hiring staff, and was directly responsible for all school operation, securing approval from the board on major changes to contracts and operations. He was also responsible for recruiting students, a necessity since the school had never experienced a waiting list or had to invoke a lottery.

THE STORY OF CULTURAL CHANGE

Describing how Clark affected the culture of the school required outlining an evolutionary process with sequential themes. These themes were *initial tensions*, *taking control*, and *a tenuous culture*.

Initial Tensions

Mr. Clark came to Kids Korner with a change agenda. He believed that he had been hired to change the school because of the vision he expressed in his interviews with the charter board. As he stated, "I was very transparent. Kids

Korner has been a good school but it's never been a great school, and after 13 years you should be a great school, and if I was bought on board that was what would be driving me . . . the end result is to change the way people do their day-to-day job and that's really where the rubber meets the road." His vision of a great school was primarily described in terms of improved academic success, as represented by improved state test scores.

Of the 48 individual codes related to Clark's interviews in the category of *principal vision*, 24 were related to state accountability testing. Similarly, of the 63 individual codes in the category *principal goals*, 42 were related to state accountability testing. In the first interview with Clark, he responded to the question, "What is your vision, overall goal for the school?" by stating, "We have to get out of two-star status . . . we need to be a three-star school by the end of [next] school year. That's pretty much a non-negotiable for me. We should have at least got up to three stars by the end of next school year." The focus on increasing state test scores did not waver throughout the three years, but was most intense in tone and volume the first year.

Clark was clear, particularly the first year, that to obtain his vision he needed to change the culture of the school. He prioritized culture shaping from the onset: "I made the board very cognizant, [school culture] isn't where it needed to be, and so that's what a lot of my efforts this summer and the beginning of the year has been, just developing the kind of culture we want." He described the culture he intended to institute as he outlined preparation for the first summer teacher professional development:

> What are we going to do this summer is to get our teachers to make sure that the kickoff of this year is strong, and it became very clear that a lot of it had to be a cultural piece. . . . Then it started, sort of big picture of expectations, and sort of what my drivers are in terms of sense of urgency, whatever it takes, no excuses. . . . To make the cultural shift on this campus where basic [state test level] really isn't good enough. We should be getting a majority of our kids at the mastery/advanced levels.

As in this statement, Clark often conflated the culture expected with improvements in state test scores. Throughout the school year, Clark continued to discuss his efforts in changing the culture of the school to a more student-achievement, test-driven culture, with a focus on no excuses in meeting goals.

In the initial interviews, teachers described the culture of the school in positive terms. When directly asked about how they would describe the culture of the school, Ms. Moyer stated, "Collaborative, everyone works together, welcoming." Mr. Wiley affirmed Moyer's description and added, "The first word that comes to mind is family. . . . I think that teachers are generally given a great deal of autonomy from curriculum all the way down to daily instruction. Teachers in the building care for kids, but also keep an eye on them." Mr. Soto, new to the school, stated, "You get support from people. Teachers care for their kids and want them to be a part of the school. Parents are really, really involved in the school."

In her fourth year at Kids Korner, Ms. Davis took on a new position as instructional coach in the first year of the study. She had worked with Clark from the early summer, planning the summer professional development focused on changing culture. She was the harbinger of the changes to come, when asked about the school culture: "Well . . . my first reaction is that it's changing. . . . I know Mr. Clark wants us to be more data-driven. . . . I think he will allow instructional freedom, but I am not sure how this emphasis will affect the kind of warm, friendly kind of welcoming culture we have had, how this will affect our relationship with kids and parents." There was clearly a mismatch between the culture desired by the principal and that described by the teachers.

By the end of the year, this mismatch became more pronounced, and clearly tension had developed between Clark's efforts to change culture and the staff's perception of the school climate and culture. As Moyer stated when asked about the school culture in the May interview: "Oh wow, it's completely . . . I'd have a completely different response now. . . . I don't want to call it 'hostile,' but it's not a positive atmosphere so much anymore." Soto, completing his first year at the school, stated, "I would say most people have been still very pleasant, but there are definitely some underlying tensions."

The teachers' interviews revealed a sense that the collaborative culture had diminished and that many of the cultural components important to the staff, such as parent involvement and a focus on students, had declined, as expressed by Wiley:

> As far as the culture of our relationship to the parents and community goes, I think that, that has maybe become less intimate. It's not a friendly environment among teachers either. We don't collaborate like we used to; there is a lot of tension in the teacher's lounge. It's like we are being pitted against each other.

Certainly, the climate had deteriorated. Even Clark recognized the climate was inhospitable in his June interview: "The climate just became so toxic that it . . . I mean, it was a horrible place." The tension among the teaching staff and Clark's pressure to change the culture and to disrupt long-valued norms was palpable in the spring interviews.

Embedded Mechanisms Employed

The principal employed a number of mechanisms to shift the culture of the school the first year. He primarily used (1) formal statements of organizational philosophy, creeds, and charter; (2) changes in organizational systems and procedures; and (3) toward the end of the year, excommunication, as defined by Schein (2010).

Clark continually and persistently communicated his philosophy of a "good school" and the kind of culture he expected in the future. Teachers in the first interview were clear that "he wants us to have a sense of urgency with getting kids, I guess, to reach their grade levels. There's this sense of urgency to be a good school" (Moyer). When asked what the principal's priorities were for the school, each teacher's first response was similar to Soto's: "I know we have certain stars we're trying to get [in the state accountability test]. I know that achievement is one." For the most part, teachers were able to articulate the general priorities set by the principal, those of becoming data-driven and focusing on student achievement.

Clark shaped the culture of the school the first year by changing a number of systems and procedures. Examples of instructional changes included requiring teachers to develop and give a pre- and post-year test and weekly assessments based on the state standards; all the assessments and results were turned into him. Clark and Davis, the instructional coach, also developed a mid-year test that mirrored the state accountability exam and had all teachers assess students. Clark expected teachers to use this test data to change instruction, but other than the initial summer professional development, he did little to provide professional support to help teachers develop skills.

Clark made other instructional changes, including requiring teachers to turn in daily lesson plans rather than weekly outlines, and requiring frequent small-group instruction each day. The principal was often in the classrooms, although he rarely gave feedback to teachers. As Soto stated at the end of the year, "He [Mr. Clark] was there close to every day; a couple of times a week minimum, even if it was just five minutes, ten minutes, pop his head in . . . never, he never gave us any feedback."

Clark also made changes related to student procedures. He instituted a no-talking and hands-folded policy in the hallways for students at the onset of school year, and changed the extended day procedures. At mid-year, he required all students to stay until 5:15 p.m. to participate in the extended day program, which had been optional for students/parents in the past. Teachers previously were paid an additional stipend for staying, but a new rotating system was put in place, and teachers were required to put in some time after school with additional pay provided beyond these assignments.

After-school programming had been mainly enrichment activities through local agencies, and some tutoring services for students. After-school activities changed to primarily tutoring and extended academic activities. Student detention for disciplinary violations was also added. At mid-year, Mr. Clark also instituted a Saturday School for both behavior issues and additional instructional tutoring. For additional pay, teachers rotated time supervising Saturday School.

The most impactful embedded mechanism related to climate and, eventually, culture was Clark's use of what Schein (2010) labels *excommunication*. Mr. Clark liberally used nonrenewal of teacher contracts as a mechanism for change. In the first interview with Clark at the beginning of the school year, he stated his intent to excommunicate those not meeting his expectations:

> Ultimately, you're going to hit a point where, this is my expectation in terms of student behavior or this is my expectation in terms of level of rigor in your classroom, and you're going to have a choice: you meet it, work hard, or you don't want to work that hard and we're going to part ways. I think there's going to be some ways parting without a doubt this summer.... I mean there's no way that all 16 teachers will be back next year.

In January, Clark told teachers in a staff meeting that if some of them didn't pick up the rigor and meet expectations, they would not be returning the following year. In March, he met individually with half the elementary teaching staff to tell them he would not be renewing their contract; one of them was Moyer, a founding teacher. Additionally, Soto and Wiley chose not to return. In total, half the teachers from the initial school year of the study did not return the second year.

Clark also decided to eliminate most of the teacher assistants, including one who had been at the school since it opened. Only two of the seven teacher assistants were hired back. Teaching assistants were one of the elements listed in the original and renewal charter to help provide a small, nurturing environment. As a result, 13 of the 24 adults who worked with students did not return. Primarily by design, Clark tried to eliminate the mismatch between his vision for the culture of the school and the existing culture through personnel changes.

Taking Control

Clark's vision of a school culture focused on high student achievement continued to drive decisions throughout the study. Although he was concerned about the negative climate at the end of his first year, he was confident that changes made at the school had resulted in a turn in school culture. When asked at the middle of the second school year how he would characterize the culture and climate of the school, he stated:

> I think we're on the right track, in the sense that academically we laid the foundations for our teachers, kids, and their families to understand what a culture of achievement is. We have sort of the foundation of teachers and kids understanding that you need to work hard.... I'm always harder on us than I

need to be, probably, but out of a 1 to 10, I'd say we were probably at, like, a 5½, 6. Better than we were the year previous, where I'd say we were at a 2½, 3.

The modest increase in school accountability scores at the end of the second year confirmed the principal's perception that the culture at Kids Korner had changed. "I think we were able to have a very good year in terms of academic achievement because we got the culture moving in the right direction."

With the exception of Davis, the instructional coach, none of the teachers interviewed the first year were still at the school in the second year of the study. During the remainder of the study, teachers were strategically selected to be interviewed. Ms. Levy was among those selected to be interviewed the second year, because she was one of the few teachers left at the school who had been there prior to Clark's arrival. She had four years of teaching experience, all of which had been at Kids Korner.

Ms. Johnson, a teacher new to the school, was selected because she had much teaching experience at several schools and took over as the instructional coach for Davis, who left after the second year of the study. Finally, Ms. Lawrence, another experienced teacher new to the school, was selected. Although the majority of the teachers who were hired over the second and third year of the study were first-year teachers, first-year teachers were intentionally not selected for interviews because of their limited background to make judgments about school culture, school structures, and procedures.

By the end of the second school year, interviewees confirmed that teachers had embraced a culture of student achievement at Kids Korner. Levy talked about the shifts in culture over the first two years of the study: "I think the morale went back up because we didn't have all that negativity everywhere, from the end of last year. Mr. Clark's ideas of student achievement and high [student accountability test] scores are what we all look for." Davis stated, "The culture and climate has changed since the first year. It is very focused on student achievement, specifically related to [student accountability test] scores and our interim assessment scores. . . . It is very driven toward improving."

The two newly hired, experienced teachers embraced the culture of the school as represented by Ms. Johnson's statement: "The first goal of the school is based on culture. We really want to build a culture of success at this school . . . everyone has a goal on how to get scores up." The descriptors of school culture from the first year, such as family, welcoming, and collaborative, had been replaced with success, achievement, and test scores.

Embedded Mechanisms Employed

Clark continued to use a variety of the culture-embedding mechanisms employed the first year to solidify the school culture he desired, including advocating for changes in organizational design and structure. However, he began to rely more on teacher recruitment and selection, in conjunction with excommunication, as primary means to strengthen the school's culture and meet his organizational goal of better student achievement. He also began to depend more heavily on allocating resources and rewards and status to shape the culture.

Clark spent much time and energy on recruiting teachers, focusing on whether the teacher could embrace expectations and the desired school culture. As he stated, "We [do] things culturally different. For us, you know, we want someone obviously that fits in with our school culture. This is what we're trying to do; do you buy into it? Do you align with our vision and our mission?"

The hiring process was rigorous and time consuming. One issue Clark faced with this hiring process was that he never had enough experienced teachers apply to the school. As a result, he tended to fall back on new teachers, primarily TFA teachers.

Even after instituting his own hiring process in his second year as principal, Clark continued to liberally excommunicate teachers if they did not meet his expectations for rigor and test score performance. He did not renew contracts for two teachers he hired the second year, and fired two teachers he hired mid-year the third year for not meeting test score goals and benchmarks, or not providing "enough rigor" during the school year.

Clark believed that the most effective way to improve student achievement was through data-driven instruction and improving data systems to support teachers' use of data. He continually advocated to the charter board for several changes to free resources to purchase programs related to data, including eliminating teacher assistants, eliminating the middle school because of low enrollment, and withdrawing from the state teacher retirement system.

With the elimination of the teaching assistants, Mr. Clark contracted with an organization that provided a program that developed cycles of benchmark tests aligned with state testing for the school. Davis was trained on how to analyze the benchmark and summative testing; she also was to redeliver the training and provide support to teachers for these cycles.

With the principal's support, the board eliminated the middle school and decided to withdraw from the state teacher retirement system at the beginning of the third year, moving all employees to matching individual retirement accounts. Clark used the funds from these changes to hire additional instructional coaches to support the high number of new teachers he anticipated having each year.

Instructionally, Mr. Clark made several structural changes. He departmentalized and instituted tracking for second through fifth grades, stating, "This will allow us to meet kids where they are academically and move those below basic [state accountability] up where they need to be." In the middle of the second year he discontinued Saturday School and mandatory after-school student participation, and focused only on low-performing students who needed tutoring programs and detention after school. He thought the cost-benefit ratio for all kids staying and for paying teachers was not worth the student achievement outcomes. He contracted with outside agencies and local nonprofits to provide tutoring services.

Clark began what he called a "teacher continuous improvement cycle process" in the third year of the study by instituting a school structure used to reward and evaluate teachers. To reward teachers, he established a bonus system based on teachers' goals related to student growth on benchmark tests. These goals were called "golden tickets." Each teacher was required to develop two or three golden ticket goals with the principal or one of the instructional coaches. The coach's bonuses were based on how well the teachers did in achieving their goals.

The golden ticket was also tied to student accountability test results, teacher evaluation, and employment, as noted by Clark: "Essentially, we gave every teacher a goal at the beginning of the year based on how his or her cohort did the year prior. These golden tickets have been updated after every benchmark and after mid-year testing. So, teachers should be very aware if they should plan on being here, and can order new staff shirts for the next year." The reward system thus complemented the principal's excommunication mechanism.

A Tenuous Culture

The final study interviews, confirmed by principal and classrooms observations, suggested a pattern of shared basic assumptions learned by the faculty. Data walls and student work were evident in every classroom. Teachers explained that student achievement gains were how things worked around Kids Korner, as noted by Levy, the only teacher who had been at Kids Korner prior to Mr. Clark: "We all really work hard on using our data to move students from basic to above basic. I think that's what we're all about here." Clark molded the assumptions shared by teachers by systematically using culture-shaping mechanisms.

The Kids Korner culture, however, appeared tenuous. At issue was the tension between stability and adaptability. The continued use of Clark's mechanisms to shape culture also appeared to be mechanisms that destabilized the organization, perhaps to the detriment of successfully reaching organization goals. By the end of the third year, a particular issue was how the principal employed the mechanisms associated with rewards and status in relation to selection, promotion, and excommunication.

Rewards and Status

The implementation of the golden ticket reward system initially met with positive responses by teachers interviewed. Teachers were highly interested in meeting these goals, and the goals did focus them on student achievement. Lawrence was one of experienced teachers who was new to Kids Korner the third year of the study. She outlined teachers' general response to the bonus structure at the beginning of the year: "I think money is motivating. We already want to improve student achievement anyway, so rewarding us—I was all in."

As the year transpired, however, perceptions of the bonuses became disconcerting to teachers because they became equated with continued employment. Johnson, the full-time instructional coach and one of three members of the administrative leadership team, articulated that the purpose of the golden ticket was not clear to even her:

> As a leadership team, we talked about the golden ticket goals, which are more lofty goals, "This is what we really need to move our [state accountability score]." So those were more "pie in the sky" kind of goals that we're looking for; but somehow they became, "This is unacceptable to us, if kids don't meet this goal." I think that that's one of my real bones of contention with the whole thing, is that I don't think it was communicated well. I don't think the teachers had a say in what was in the golden ticket goals. I think they see them as a "gotcha."

Johnson continued to discuss how the pressure of the golden ticket was affecting teachers: "It [golden ticket] sends the wrong message. When I have my best teacher say to me, 'Every day I feel like I'm getting punched in the stomach because I'm not meeting one of those goals,' it sends the wrong message."

Clark, however, thought that the golden ticket was setting expectations for teacher performance and expectations for employment: "Using a very corporate-like system here, where there is no gray area . . . you make your goal or you don't. Teachers should be doing this anyway—but if for some reason a teacher doesn't care about data, and isn't obsessed with it, and always looking at it, there's no excuse why he or she shouldn't be gone." The bonus system reinforced the culture desired by principal for high student achievement and data-driven instruction, but it also created other issues related to stabilizing the culture, setting what Ms. Lawrence called "churn and turn for teachers."

Clark intentionally used teacher "churn and turn" as a means to achieve his cultural expectations by not renewing and firing teachers who did not meet his expectations. He made intense efforts to find teachers who would follow his lead as far as expectations and culture. However, this piece of the culture interfered with the principal's goals related to increased student achievement. As Johnson explained:

> I think you have to build relationships with people. As the [state accountability score] goes up if you do not retain people . . . you're not going to get past certain humps. You need good teachers and retain what they learn this year and build upon that the next year and so on and so on; otherwise you're never going to increase—you're going to reach a plateau and you're going to get stuck there. So when he says, "Well, we'll just get three TFA teachers to fill these holes," I say, "Remember, TFA teachers are going home because they're from Massachusetts and Rhode Island and California."

Both Johnson and Lawrence thought the principal's solution to culture building was to hire his way into performance. Lawrence stated:

> He [Mr. Clark] doesn't see the need to build relationships. We are all kind of widgets, replaceable. It's like, "We want you to work harder because you, you've done well, so we want you to work even harder. And if you're not willing to work even harder, despite what you've done this year, then we'll just replace you."

Throughout the study, teachers related their interactions with Clark as "businesslike," "distant," "unrealistic," and "unappreciative." In several cases, they expressed fear.

The decision to withdraw from the teacher retirement system exacerbated the turnover issues and the potential recruiting and selection of teachers. Mr. Clark had intentionally recruited Johnson and Lawrence in the third year of the study to be full- and part-time instructional coaches. Both teachers had histories of outstanding student performance, and both had experience in coaching teachers. Both were vested in the teacher retirement system, and had come to Kids Korner with the understanding that they would continue in the system. Both said they would not be returning, nor would they have come if they had known that Kids Korner was withdrawing from the retirement system. It was clear to teachers that the chances of recruiting experienced teachers at Kids Korner would be limited, since the school was no longer in the system.

When asked about the challenges of new teachers, the possibility of losing experienced teachers, and the possibility of hiring experienced teachers in the future without the retirement system, Clark explained all in cost-benefit terms:

> Financially, it's essentially a zero-sum. I haven't really drawn many veteran teachers here, even with [teacher retirement system]. I think that decision only solidified the fact that we will always be in this: our length of year, our length of day, our expectations, and the fact that we're an at-will employer. I think

those have always, sort of, weeded out teachers that have a lot more experience.

Although Clark had expressed the need to support new teachers, in no interview over the three years did he discuss the need to retain teachers. The word *retain* or phrases such as "keep teachers" did not appear in any of Clark's interviews. The high teacher turnover and continued use of mechanisms that created instability may have created a culture that was unsustainable and unable to support the goals set by the principal for student achievement. In the end, Clark left the school after the third year to take a job in the SDOE.

SUMMARY

The culture that Clark developed over the three years was radically different from that when he arrived. From the onset of his tenure, Clark was clear about the kind of culture he wanted for the school, and was intentional about using mechanisms that he believed would lead to that culture. When he arrived, teachers described the culture as one focused on collaboration and supporting students and parents. At the end of the study, Clark and teacher participants described the culture in terms outlined by the principal, a culture with "a sense of urgency, whatever it takes, no excuses," driven by data to improve student achievement. The continued reliance on mechanisms that change organizational culture by destabilizing it may have also led to a form of dysfunction that prevented Clark from reaching his primary goal of improved student achievement.

Although Mr. Clark believed teachers and the school community had embraced his vision for the culture of the school by the third year, he was not satisfied with student achievement outcomes. As a result, he continued to excommunicate teachers and staff each year, use rewards in the form of bonuses tied to employment, and shift organizational systems and procedures to achieve his goal at the expense of stabilizing the culture he had developed. Besides developing a culture focused on student achievement, Clark had also established a culture of "churn and turn" in terms of faculty and organizational systems and procedures. There was little staff continuity or continuity in school systems or structures that could lead to stabilizing programs, curriculum, and instruction.

Throughout the three years, Clark's interactions with teachers were more characteristic of transactional leadership than transformational leadership. Clark laid out specific tasks and provided rewards for achieving the task. Needs of followers were subsidiary to the principal's expectations, and he relied on corrective actions when performance deviated from those expectations. Correctives tended to be in the form of negative feedback or disciplinary action. Rather than inspiring motivation or supporting innovation, Clark's interactions with followers seemed to generate fear.

IMPLICATIONS FOR PRACTICE

This single case study is a cautionary tale about principal change and culture in a charter school rather than an outline of charter school leadership in general. The findings from this research suggest questions to ponder for researchers, policy makers, and practitioners. What happened at Kids Korner opens questions about organizational goals, governance, autonomy, and how principals understand culture and the process of cultural change in charter schools.

One of the limitations of this study was not including the perceptions of charter board members. From Clark's perspective, he was hired by the board specifically to create change. It is unclear if this was the case, but the board granted Clark much autonomy in how he used mechanisms to shape the culture. One of the important aspects of charter schools is the autonomy given them with regard to rules and regulations, which allows them to be nimble in adapting to the environment and leading innovation through change. This autonomy was extended to Clark, who used it to make major organizational changes. By the end of the third year, he had changed the school culture, including members' understanding of the school mission and vision outlined in the charter.

The principal also changed and eliminated school structures outlined in the existing charter related to the mission of the school. It appeared that the charter no longer guided organizational goals or the culture meant to achieve those goals. The direction of the school seemed to be that of Clark's vision and mission, and not that set by the charter or the governing board. The question becomes, what was the board's role in balancing the stability outlined in the charter with the autonomy given the principal to adapt and innovate through cultural change.

Kids Korner was not the same school at the end of the three-year study as it was at the beginning. It had been reborn. At issue, however, was the new principal's continued use of turnaround strategies rather than shifting to strategies that could stabilize the fragile culture he developed. Throughout the three years, Clark made quick and rapid changes, employing mechanisms that destabilized culture, and particularly relying on excommunication, rewarding compliance, and changing fundamental school processes and structures, even though it appeared he had gained a school culture focused on student achievement.

A growing body of research suggests that school cultures that are more likely to increase student achievement foster a shared commitment to excellence, are collaborative, and value the people that positively contribute to the organization (Gruenert, 2005; Hoy & Hannum, 1997; Louis et al., 2010). Mr. Clark's ultimate organizational goal was high student achievement, and he appeared to have developed a shared commitment to that goal. However, his actions did not foster a culture of collaboration, nor did he foster a culture in which people were valued. He instead fostered a culture in which people—teachers and staff—were expendable, a toxic culture, according to Gruenert and Whitaker (2015).

Even in the change process, Gruenert and Whitaker (2015) outlined the importance of people in developing culture, suggesting that "when pursuing cultural change, we need to make sure that we always protect the most valuable people in the organization" (p. 109). By continuing to foster a culture of "churn and turn" with respect to staff, Clark was in a continuous cycle of spending energy in building culture rather than using a stable, healthy culture to attain goals. The question arises as to whether this new and inexperienced principal was unwilling to, or did not know when or how to, stabilize the organization to meet these goals. This is particularly true with respect to collaboration and retaining teachers. A lesson learned may be that principals with greater autonomy need to understand when to destabilize cultures for change and innovation, and when and how to temper change with elements of stability.

REFERENCES

Alvesson, M. (2011). Leadership and organizational culture. In A. Bryman, D. Collinson, K. Grint, B. Jackson, & Uhl-Bien (Eds.), *The Sage handbook of leadership* (pp. 151–164). Thousand Oaks, CA: Sage.

Bass, B. M., & Avolio, B. J. (1993). Transformational leadership and organizational culture. *Public administration quarterly*, 112–121.

Bass, B. M., & Avolio, B. J. (1994). *Transformational leadership: Improving organizational effectiveness*. Thousand Oaks, CA: Sage.

Bolman, L. G., & Deal, T. E. (2013). *Reframing organizations: Artistry, choice, and leadership*. San Francisco: Jossey-Bass.

Collins, K. M. T., Onwuegbuzie, A. J., & Jiao, Q. G. (2007). A mixed methods investigation of mixed methods sampling designs in social and health science research. *Journal of Mixed Methods Research, 1*(3), 267–294. doi:10.1177/1558689807299526

Creswell, J. W. (2013). *Qualitative inquiry and research design: Choosing among five approaches* (3rd ed.). Thousand Oaks, CA: Sage.

Deal, T. E., & Peterson, K. D. (1999). *Shaping school culture: The heart of leadership* (1st ed.). San Francisco: Jossey-Bass.

Deal, T. E., & Peterson, K. D. (2010). *Shaping school culture: Pitfalls, paradoxes, and promises*. Hoboken, NJ: John Wiley & Sons.

Edmonds, R. R. (1979). Effective schools for the urban poor. *Educational Leadership, 37*(1), 15–24.

Gruenert, S. (2005). Correlations of collaborative school cultures with student achievement. *NASSP Bulletin, 89*(645), 43–55.

Gruenert, S., & Whitaker, T. (2015). *School culture rewired: How to define, assess, and transform it*. Alexandria, VA: ASCD.

Hall, G. E., & George, A. A. (1999). The impact of principal change facilitator style on school and classroom culture. In H. Jerome Freiberg (Ed.), *School climate: Measuring, improving, and sustaining healthy learning environments* (pp. 165–185). London: Falmer Press. 1999.

Hoy, W. K., & Hannum, J. W. (1997). Middle school climate: An empirical assessment of organizational health and student achievement. *Educational Administration Quarterly, 33*(3), 290–311. doi:10.1177/0013161X97033003003

Leithwood, K., & Jantzi, D. (1990). Transformational leadership: How principals can help reform school cultures. *School effectiveness and school improvement, 1*(4), 249–280.

Leithwood, K., & Jantzi, D. (2000). The effects of transformational leadership on organizational conditions and student engagement with school. *Journal of Educational Administration, 38*(2), 112–129.

Louis, K. S., Leithwood, K., Wahlstrom, K. L., Anderson, S. E., Michlin, M., Gordon, M., . . . Moore, S. (2010). *Learning from leadership: Investigating the links to improved student learning: Final report of research findings*. Minneapolis, MN and Toronto: Wallace Foundation. Retrieved from http://www.wallacefoundation.org/knowledge-center/Documents/Investigating-the-Links-to-Improved-Student-Learning.pdf

Lubienski, C. A., & Weitzel, P. C. (Eds.). (2010). *The charter school experiment: Expectations, evidence, and implications*. Cambridge, MA: Harvard Education Press.

Merseth, K. K. (2009). *Inside urban charter schools*. Cambridge, MA: Harvard Education Press.

Northouse, P. G. (2013). *Leadership: Theory and practice*. Thousand Oaks, CA: Sage.

Patton, M. Q. (2002). *Qualitative research and evaluation methods* (3rd ed.). Thousand Oaks, CA: Sage.

Purkey, S. C., & Smith, M. S. (1982). Too soon to cheer? Synthesis of research on effective schools. *Educational Leadership, 40*(3), 64–69.

Saldaña, J. (2013). *The coding manual for qualitative researchers* (2nd ed.). Los Angeles: Sage.

Sammons, P. (1995). *Key characteristics of effective schools: A review of school effectiveness research*. London: B & MBC Distribution Services.

Schein, E. H. (2010). *Organizational culture and leadership, vol. 2*. Hoboken, NJ: John Wiley & Sons.

Stake, R. E. (2006). *Mutliple case study analysis*. New York: Guilford Press.

Wohlstetter, P., Smith, J., & Farrell, C. (2013). *Choices and challenges: Charter school performance in perspective*. Cambridge, MA: Harvard Education Press.

Yin, R. K. (2009). *Case study research: Design and methods* (4th ed.). Los Angeles: Sage.

Yin, R. K. (2012). *Applications of case study research*. Thousand Oaks, CA: Sage.

Chapter Five

Transformative Charter School Leaders

Tempered Radicalism in Practice

Linsay DeMartino

THE CHEETOS STORY

"Power-over" administration does not initiate school change. However, it does begin with the administrative team using "power-with" strategies, such as developing authentic relationships with the school community. According to Yolanda Wright, cofounder and director of college and career readiness at Millennium High School, "We do things that break down those things in a traditional power hierarchy. When we go to [the camp grounds] together, we are all wearing t-shirts and jeans, hanging out on the bus, and eating Cheetos together—that is a real leveler."

Yolanda went on to say,

> You can't then turn around and put on a suit and act all superior to kids after you have sat in the dirt with them and say, "Pass those Cheetos." It's just that you have already established this connection that you are all real people. If you were going to suit up, you are going to have to do it in the most respectful and compassionate way. You don't get to then start bossing kids around in an artificial way. It doesn't work. The kids have already seen you sit in the dirt with them.

Through Yolanda's story, by using tempered means in the form of authentic relationship building, the transformative leader becomes an agent of educational change.

AN INTRODUCTION TO THE CHARTER SCHOOL MOVEMENT

In the 1980s, the concept of charter schools was developed by Albert Shanker (1988) as a response to increasing disparities in educational attainment across schools. As learning laboratories of advanced educational pathways, Shanker believed teacher- and community-driven schools would house diverse student populations (Lubienski & Weitzel, 2010). To lessen the educational opportunity gap through educator autonomy, teachers were looking to create smaller, personalized, and relevant schools to serve lower socioeconomic communities (Fabricant & Fine, 2015). These burgeoning charter schools were mostly started and run by educators, resulting in a movement inspired by deregulation and innovation.

From the beginning of the movement, charter schools have been driven by a system of deregulation. According to Vergari (1999), charter schools have the liberty to "make their own decisions regarding matters such as personnel, curricula, and contracting for services. Autonomy in decision making permits charter school managers to employ new education delivery mechanisms that might prove superior to those commonly used by the school district" (p. 391). Since bureaucratic structures in public school districts have contributed to the destruction of clear educative goals that best serve all students, charter schools are meant to provide free education without the bureaucracy usually associated with traditional public schools.

By using innovative practices, proponents of the movement argue that charter schools are more effective than traditional public schools. As such, charter schools are a "mechanism for students seeking to improve the quality of their own education but also engender competition that will lead to improvements in the quality of education for students who remain in traditional public schools" (Sass, 2006, p. 92). In this way, innovation must include alternative pathways to school leadership, such as the use of transformative leadership practices.

Charter schools were originally established as acts of social justice (Fabricant & Fine, 2015). For example, instead of learning in overpopulated classrooms with irrelevant curriculum, most charter schools offer a smaller, more personalized environment for students. These charter schools are referred to as community-based institutions (CBIs). They are typically educator driven, and more likely to respond directly to the educational needs of the community. Finally, as a result of these former benefits, charter schools typically attract and hire more effective teachers. These teachers typically have expanded opportunities for leadership in program design and decision-making.

On the other hand, opponents of the charter school movement claim that the neoliberal agenda, or the corporatization and marketization of schooling, is driving this movement in the name of educational reform. First, charter management organizations (CMOs), which are nonprofit charter organizations, have created hybrid management structures (Huerta & Zuckerman, 2009). In other words, corporate and local offices share control of school structures. Mirrored structures, including vision, mission, top-down leadership, and standards-based curriculum, are modeled after the traditional public school.

Next, educational management organizations (EMOs) are for-profit management companies, most often national companies, which exclusively run regional charter schools. These charters grant less autonomy, eliminate authentic community control, consider schooling to be a business, and view parents and guardians as consumers (Dixson, Royal, & Lawrence Henry, 2013). These schools are often exclusionary to certain types of students (i.e., students with disabilities and students who score poorly on entrance exams and/or standardized tests) and extremely competitive (Huerta & Zuckerman, 2009). However, these exclusionary practices and competition are often presented under the guise of "academic excellence."

With the influx CMO and EMO charter schools, schools are becoming decentralized; however, through these efforts, the policy making and governance of schools are in the hands of non-educators. Corporate America has become increasingly interested in contemporary charter schools. The corporate movement is "associated with a relentless attack on teachers and teacher unions, the ideological critique of public education as in 'crisis,' and consequent seductive advertisements for families to exit the public sector" (Fabricant & Fine, 2015, p. 2). In this way, corporate America is overtaking leadership in schools.

Due to this change in educational leadership, common critiques declare that resources are being drained and the academic elite are being siphoned away from traditional public schools, resulting in a rise of racial, ethnic, and class-based school segregation (Cobb & Glass, 1999; Fabricant & Fine, 2015; Sass, 2006). Therefore, since there is still a need for an independent and individualized approach to education, it is essential to differentiate between charter schools, which continue to run as acts of social justice, and the schools within the charter school movement, which are part of the neoliberal agenda.

Clearly, not all charter schools are the same; thus, it is not helpful to aggregate them together. To acknowledge the fact that grassroots resistance in public education is still thriving, it is important to differentiate certain charter schools, such as the charter school from my study, from the charter school movement. According to Fabricant and Fine (2015), coalitions of educators, parents, youth, and other community stakeholders "must win back the identity of critic, reformer, and innovator" (p. 128). The return of progressive CBIs create a framework for educational change through proactive educational agendas, such as educational quality, equitable access, smaller class sizes, culturally conscious educators, and community involvement.

Contemporary Charter Schools

Across the United States, there are more than 6,800 charter schools serving nearly 3 million children. This represents a substantial and rapid increase from the 4,000 charter schools that served more than 1 million students in 2007 (Center for Education Reform, 2016). Some contemporary charter schools are, in fact, innovative and progressive. In these schools, administrative leadership plays an important role in shifting conventional and bureaucratic public schooling to a more organic and supportive school community that includes ethnically, racially, and linguistically diverse members. These are schools in which educational leaders challenge traditional conceptions of leadership by using alternative practices.

In this chapter, which draws from an 18-month critical ethnographic study located in a southwestern urban charter school, I examine the use of transformative leadership practices and tempered radicalism as mechanisms to revitalize educational leadership. More specifically, the transformative school leadership at Millennium High School are "tempered radicals," defined as leaders who take deliberate and incremental actions that contribute to the dismantling of traditional power-over leadership strategies. Therefore, the purpose of this chapter is to investigate *how* transformative charter school leaders, as tempered radicals, operate and become community agents of change.

TRANSFORMATIVE LEADERSHIP: AN EMPIRICAL REVIEW

Due to bureaucratic restraints, such as irrelevant curriculum and overwhelming testing mandates, historically marginalized students are victims of inadequate and inequitable education; therefore, traditional educational leadership is outdated. Leadership cannot be determined by a formula because this ignores dimensions of culture, politics, and power. Therefore, "transformative leadership begins with questions of justice and democracy; it critiques inequitable practices and offers the promise not only of greater individual achievement but of a better life lived in common with others" (Shields, 2010a, p. 559). Put differently, transformative leadership is educational leadership for a pluralistic society through inclusivity and socially just learning.

To further defy traditional educational leadership practices, transformative leadership is based in community collaboration. Within the context of democratic thought, "leaders are led, just as those who are led are leaders" (Weiner, 2003, p. 96). By avoiding power-over techniques often used by school administrators, the school becomes based in positive relationships among all stakeholders. In addition, "the common elements in these transformative approaches include the need for social betterment, enhancing equity, and for a thorough reshaping of knowledge and belief structures" (Shields, 2010b, p. 28). Thus, by adopting these former tenets, the school begins to act as a community.

Borrowing from Foster's (1986) transformative leadership theory, the framework is comprised of four components: transformational, ethical, educative, and critical. Transformative leadership "demands that educational leaders critically assess the asymmetrical relations of power in the organizational context and deconstruct . . . those practices and cultural artifacts that engender an anti-democratic discourse in organizations such as schools" (Dantley, 2003, p. 15). Through critical interpretation, school leaders transform their practice through the reconstruction of social creations based on race, class, gender, language, ability, and/or sexual orientation.

THEORETICAL FRAMEWORK: TRANSFORMATIVE LEADERSHIP

Transformative leaders believe the meaning of schooling "as primarily concerned with the individual as a member of the polity; education serves to liberate . . . to give the individual an image of a complete and wholesome society" (Foster, 1988, p. 69). A transformative leader considers the school environment while continuing to value everyone. She or he places value on diversity beyond racial and ethnic differentiations. There must be questioning of the status quo by reflecting on the past and continually assessing traditions for injustices and inequities. Through conceptualizing school leadership by using transformational, ethical, educative, and critical dimensions, the entire school will invest in challenging normalized schooling practices.

Transformational Dimension

Administrative practice as a transformational dimension[1] is the foundation for building and sustaining an educational community. Instead of power-wielding leadership practices, administrative behaviors transform. The behaviors aim to achieve empowerment, equity, and excellence for all school community members, and individualized expertise must be valued throughout the school.

The transformational school leader acknowledges the various skills, knowledges, and capabilities among their school community. By confirming these former community attributes as valuable, relationship and trust building ensues, resulting in a power-with educational atmosphere. Next, an important component of the transformative leadership framework is ethical practices.

Ethical Dimension

Educational leadership must encompass moral practice. As such, it is important for school leaders to acknowledge that "education exists in a real world populated by real agents who occupy positions of power and who use and abuse power" (Foster, 1989, p. 16). School administrators must balance the political, economic, and social relationships that exist within the school and larger school community. Two examples of balancing these relationships include open communication in the form of honest discussions and dialogue, and acknowledgment of successes in the form of public acknowledgments within the school community.

Educative Dimension

The educative school administrator is an agent of empowerment. Although awareness of self contributes to empowerment, "leadership in education settings involves the empowerment of followers through engaging in a mutual vision oriented toward end values, such as freedom and equality" (Foster, 1989, p. 11). School leaders focus on common needs and work together with other stakeholders to meet those needs. Put differently, administrative practice becomes a collaborative effort for mutual goodwill among all school stakeholders. Like the educative administrator, there is leadership for critical awareness.

Critical Dimension

Equitable educational opportunities exist within and outside the school day. In fact, critical administrators are leaders for social justice and equity. Leadership for social justice and equity is achieved by conscientization, reflection, and dialogue (Freire, 1970). Conscientization is a realization of the immediate and surrounding world around us. According to Freire (1970), through this realization, in order to "perceive social, political, and economic contradictions, and to take action against the oppressive elements of reality" (p. 19), alternative, transformative pedagogies must be considered. Therefore, critical leaders embrace realism and encourage their community to contribute to the dismantling of the status quo.

In sum, transformative administrators consistently use transformational, ethical, educative, and critical dimensions in their leadership within their school communities. The transformational dimension incorporates equitable empowering strategies disseminated throughout the entire school community. The ethical leader acknowledges the hierarchal structure that exists within the school community. As an educative school administrator, it is important to provide a historical narrative to reveal the true nature of oppression. The critical leader encourages agency among faculty, staff, and students. Along the same lines, transformative leaders induce change efforts through tempered means.

AN OVERVIEW OF TEMPERED RADICALISM

Caution and commitment are underlying characteristics associated with transformative leaders. However, the desire to change a school district program, a school policy, or a departmental custom can be through revolutionary or incremental actions (Meyerson, 2003). Educators who seek change through patient and persistent actions are called tempered radicals.

Therefore, transformative leaders do not have to be brisk and extreme in their actions; as such, tempered radicals deliberately prompt change through their commitment, and are typically gradual and undramatic (Meyerson, 2003). Since tempered radicals work within an existing system, they "struggle between their desire to act on their 'different' selves and the need to fit in to the dominant culture" (Meyerson, 2003, p. 5). By probing current practices and seeking alternative pathways, the different selves create a new system of learning, knowing, and change.

Since the values and beliefs are typically more progressive than the dominant ways of thinking, tempered radicals are "tempered" because they endure a process of heating and cooling, resulting in the eventual dismantling of the status quo (Meyerson, 2003). Therefore, tempered radicals frequently shift from navigating the middle ground to using anger to fuel the building of strength and cohesiveness for their desired change.

On the other hand, tempered radicals do not fit the common definition of "radical." Radicals advocate for extreme measures. However, tempered radicals push back on popular conventions through steady, deliberate acts and negotiations to shift the consciousness of others from within their organizations. They wish to use tempered methods and strategies as part of the organization, rather than from outside it.

Therefore, tempered radicalism is defined as any action performed by the administrator, inside and outside of her or his job duties, that contributes to the dismantling of traditional power structures and the building of a sustainable school community. Furthermore, through the consistent use of tempered strategies and transformative leadership practices, including transformational, ethical, educative, and critical leadership dimensions, school administrators have the potential to become transformative-tempered radicals.

RESEARCH METHODOLOGY

The purpose of this critical ethnography is to challenge traditional power-over conceptions of leadership and to explore innovative charter school transformative leadership through tempered means. Since this method is "based on critical epistemology, not on value orientations" (Carspecken, 1996, p. 22), this study is approached with beliefs in multiple truths grounded in the individual actor's personalized experiences. More specifically, the focus is on unique power-with relationships between the administrative team and the larger school community.

Various actors reported that this school actively involves faculty, staff, students, and other community members in the decision-making process, including untraditional pedagogy, globally oriented curriculum, and inclusive campus policies. Therefore, since "particular settings, persons, or activities [were] selected deliberately to provide information that is particularly relevant to [the study's] questions and goals," a purposive sample was used (Maxwell, 2013, p. 97). Thus, this 18-month critical ethnographic study took place at Millennium High School.

The larger study consisted of four phases of research: (1) administrative team, (2) faculty and staff, (3) students, and (4) parents and community stakeholders. This chapter primarily draws from the first and second research phases. By using a critical point of view and an inductive process (Madison, 2012), participant observations and interviews were analyzed for overarching themes.

First, through the initial pass of the transcripts, intuitive and undifferentiated low-level coding emerged. Then, meaning was brought to the observed actions using Carspecken's (1996) horizontal analysis to find importance beyond mere words. Finally, the codes were verified and categorized to see patterns, gaps, and themes.

For purposes of this study, I was sensitive to what I was noticing, why I was noticing it, and the interpretation of what I was noticing. Finally, I enlisted others to provide feedback. In this way, crystallization techniques were used for trustworthiness (Glesne, 2011). To achieve conclusive evidence, three points of view were used in this study: archival data, participant observations, and multiple interviews. For purposes of validity, member checking was used after the transcription of the interviews to see if findings were accurate.

Demographics of the School Community

Millennium High School was a visionary development of the need for small and intimate educational experiences for students, hands-on exploration of place-based education, project-based learning, and college readiness. The three cofounders, Sara Thomas, Charles Hill, and Yolanda Wright, sought a downtown location, as they believed it to be the hub of the city.

The framework, timeline, and opening for Millennium High School was set for the 1999–2000 school year; however, the school did not open until fall

2004. The school opened initially for ninth and tenth graders only. The downtown location of the school provided the perfect catalyst for the educational philosophy of the small school, place-based learning, and the merging of curriculum and real-world issues. Based on its geographic location, to bring sense of place and relevancy to the educational experience, students visit the surrounding downtown community, including university resources, museums, theater, art spaces, historic neighborhoods, and centers of government.

The administrative team at Millennium High School are Sara Thomas, who serves as executive director and former principal; Charles Hill, who serves as principal and former lead teacher; Yolanda Wright, who serves as director of college and career readiness and former principal/lead teacher; and Dean Smith, who serves as assistant principal/dean of students and former teacher. The 25 part- and full-time faculty and staff are not as diverse as in years past, and currently are predominately white. In aggregate, over time, the demographics of the student population are 45–55 percent white, 40–45 percent Latino, with Asian American, African American, and Native American each comprising another 5 percent.

FINDINGS

The Lore of Millennium High School

This story behind Millennium High School is best told by an eyewitness. According to Yolanda, the school was "just born out of the friendship of the three cofounders [who worked at the same traditional public school]. . . . We just started having ideas, dreams about opening our own school. Which I think is pretty common for most educators . . . if I could open up my own school and then we just got serious about it and thought, why not." As educators living in the southwestern United States, there was a lot of charter school activity going on.

After the cofounders began the process of opening a charter school, Yolanda went on to say, "We had a lot of conversations, the legend changes depending on who you talk to, but it always involves a hike or a camping trip, we were kind of out there, spending time as friends and our conversations were always, always about: What would we do? What would the school year look like? What kind of curriculum?"

Yolanda, Sara, and Charles were colleagues who shared a common vision of a more student-centered school. The catalyst for the evolution of Millennium High School began with the current situation in their former public school. Yolanda stated:

> [Our school] was the opposite of this really rigid—class, class, class—you know, lots of kids in these big schools. It felt pretty impersonalized. The curriculum just felt really disconnected to what the kids were really interested in. . . .The kids seem just so formulaic in what they wanted, and they were not very creative, and it was because we were not cultivating them as educators.

In 2001, the cofounders came up with a timeline for the school. In 2001, there was a sticky note that Sara had. It indicated that she was going to go get her advanced degree, start planning, and open the school in 2003. With advanced and intricate planning, the school opened in 2004. In addition to the unique story of the conception of Millennium High School, my findings indicate that the leadership team are transformative-tempered radicals.

The Transformative-Tempered Radical: Transformational

The transformational leader contributes to the empowerment of the faculty and staff, students, and community. At Millennium High School, the leadership team applied various transformational-tempered strategies to provide a school culture devoted to equity and excellence. These tempered properties include faculty and staff leadership groups; positive relationships among faculty, staff, and students; the student advisory program; and continued interactions with parents/guardians and community members.

First, the incorporation of valued faculty and staff leadership groups, such as the student success team (SST) and division team meetings, contributed to the trust building and empowerment within the school building. I had the opportunity to observe meetings between the members of the SST team. The team is made up of faculty and staff, including the principal, counselor, assistant principal, director of college and career readiness, registrar, and the after-school programs coordinator.

During my observation, Charles provided agendas for the meetings. The agenda consisted of the names of students in need of interventions. After the student's name was given, the team discussed past, present, and future interventions for that particular student. According to Dean, "It's combining student life and academics . . . and I think it's just looking at all the factors that contribute to student success." After a planned amount of time, the team moved on to the next student, and the process repeated. While discussions occurred, another member took copious notes to be transferred to a spreadsheet. This documentation was shared with all faculty and staff.

Charles stated that division team meetings are "when teachers discuss first what's going well [or] who is doing a great job, because I want to open those STT meetings with some positives. Kids don't really improve unless they are being told what they're doing right." By opening the meetings positively, Charles deliberately engages in transformational-tempered strategies. Division team meetings are a weekly event in which groups of grades nine/ten and eleven/twelve teachers discuss students and pedagogy.

Next, school personnel and student relationships are an important part of the school culture at Millennium High School. When you walk into Millennium High School, there is an overwhelming feeling of togetherness. Student artwork, senior personal statements, school awards and, most importantly, smiling students, faculty, and staff welcome visitors at the door.

When asked about the importance of building student relationships, Charles stated, "Our focus is this, I wanted to kind of build on the strength that we have, that is, building relationships with students—but then taking that next step and leveraging, or making full use of those relationships to translate into student learning and achievement." Also, Sara noted,

> We are an exceptionally caring environment, where every single individual is known as an individual. . . . So keeping ourselves small enough so we could be that sort of the garden of learning. . . . [Within this environment], every opportunity should be a mentorship-type opportunity, or adults modeling how to be your best adult self."

Along the same lines, Yolanda correlated the size of the school with relationships and student success. Since Millennium is a small school, she said:

> [There is an] informality, a familiarity, a comfort level between teachers and students that just simply cannot exist in a large traditional high school. I think that familiarity and family at that comfort level with each other is what gives way to pretty much everything that is great about [our school].

Relationship building between administrators, faculty, staff, and students builds authenticity and trust among all constituents. Yolanda also stated:

> The fact that we have a higher graduation rate than the state, the fact that we have a lower dropout rate than the state, the fact that our numbers—not through a letter grade, and not the testing that's not going to be an indication of our relationships—but getting kids to stick it out, getting first-generation, college-bound kids to apply and go to college, that is all born out of the fact that we have relationships.

In other words, due to the size of the school, the faculty and staff cultivated their relationships with students and leveraged student success.

In addition, the inclusion of student advisory groups contributed to the transformational foundation at the school. Advisory was included in the master schedule three times per week. For advisory, students were matched with faculty and/or staff advisors at the onset of their enrollment at Millennium

High School. Students remained with the same advisor for the duration of their time at the school.

During my time at Millennium High School, I observed three different advisory groups. The advisory groups acted as families within the larger school community. Accordingly, Dean stated, "You really get to know the students and the families, the back stories, and then that relationship . . . [becomes] pretty positive. It's rare when we end up switching advisories because that relationship becomes a real support for the kids and a real insight for the staff."

Finally, the continuous involvement of parents/guardians and community members is an integral part of the sustainable school community. Family nights occur at the school every Thursday evening. During my observations, the planned activities included healthy cooking demonstrations, student art shows, college nights, and family yoga events. In addition, parents are expected to attend student roundtables, a planned nonhierarchical parent-student-teacher conference.

For community involvement, Dean stated, "We are very able and willing to go out in the community and . . . are very immersed in their own little communities and bring the community to school." Sara furthered this statement by emphasizing the important relationship between community partnerships and the school curriculum by "bringing in community partners, getting kids out to community partners, getting kids out to field trips—really trying to make our school part of a hub of other educational organizations and institutions."

By using faculty and staff leadership groups; positive relationships among faculty, staff, and students; the student advisory program; and continued interactions with parents/guardians and community members, the administrative team at Millennium High Schooling consistently used transformational-tempered strategies. These deliberate and incremental changes contributed to "flipping the script" at the school as the traditional power-over transformed into power-with regarding school stakeholders.

The Transformative-Tempered Radical: Ethical

At Millennium High School, the administrative team acted with moral soundness as they openly embraced the faculty, staff, and students by maintaining open communication. By using this tempered means, trust ensued. Thus, a lack of divisiveness was achieved among the administrative team and community stakeholders. Charles explained, "There is a level of trust that I feel at the school. There are not a lot of conversations that go on, hopefully, that are negative that I don't know about. There doesn't seem to be a lot of, you know, divisiveness between staff and administration, and administration and students."

Also, during my observations, faculty, staff, and students seemed happy to be at school. In my experience, after last bell, everyone is ready to run out the door. This never happened at Millennium. Faculty, staff, and students typically stayed after school to complete homework, participate in activities, or chat.

Another tempered change maker was the incorporation of a student voice committee. The intention of the student voice committee was like a traditional student council; however, one distinguishing factor was that the student committee members could review new school policies.

For instance, Dean brought the new cell phone policy to a weekly meeting. The proposed cell phone policy was typical: it addressed times of use, classroom expectations, emergencies, implementation, etiquette, and consequences. During discussion of the policy, students expressed their concerns over millennial cultural differences, including the phone as a learning tool, as a non-distractor, and as an emergency contact. As a result of this meeting, the cell phone policy was amended to include cell phone use in certain situations and under teacher discretion.

The leadership team also established the Habits of Heart and Mind to acknowledge student successes. The Habits of Heart and Mind were derived from Meier's (2002) work at Central Park East. According to Sara,

> The Habits of Heart and Mind just sort of add that real-world layer. [They try] to get us out of the silos of different subject areas . . . [to] just help students become metacognitive. [With this] you can see the bigger picture, getting all the students up to 30,000 feet to investigate their own learning and what the connections are.

Sara went on to say, "The Habits of Heart and Mind help with that. You could use other names, like a lifelong learner, or attributes of a learner or . . . but just really getting kids to think about that more—the meta-level of learning. I think it helps." In addition, Dean noted that 72 percent of the kids last year "were awarded a Habit of Heart and Mind in front of the whole school . . . we give awards based on if the staff or student sees if a kid is doing something extraordinary . . . then at whole-school meeting we hand them out, and everyone recognizes them and claps."

Since the attainment of knowledge is an ongoing process, by incorporating the Habits of Heart and Mind into the school culture, the ethical transformative-tempered radical administrative team made a clear decision to embrace and celebrate the fact that the attainment of knowledge is a lifelong journey.

The Transformative-Tempered Radical: Educative

The administrative team fell short of educative leadership actions. The emphasis on the critical friends group (CFG) for faculty and staff provided the foundation for a meaningful professional learning opportunity. Yolanda said that in CFG, "we build trust. It is an overt protocol that we follow where we are setting norms, building trust, and then we are sharing our most challenging work with colleagues and asking them for help . . . we are creating just some real powerful collegiality." However, there was no evidence that difficult educationally based discussions around race, gender, sexuality, and class were occurring in these meetings. Similarly, the faculty and staff coaching was emerging in their development as educational professionals.

As educative transformative-tempered radicals, the use of an innovative curriculum assisted in their development as educational professionals. The emphasis on project-based and place-based learning contributed to the education of the whole student. The most profound example of this was a geometry project-based assignment. For this project, geometric and engineering properties were used for the construction of kites. At the same time, the project deliberately contributed to the dismantling of the status quo, as the kites spread awareness for transgender youth in the immediate community.

Also, in terms of place-based learning, Yolanda stated, "We have a commitment to place-based learning. . . . If they are studying an issue, we look at it at a local level, if something is happening in the community we try to get the kids out. We try to use local resources." During my observations, I accompanied the science class to the wetlands, a local water treatment facility and wildlife habitat. During this trip to the outdoor classroom, students were able to engage with personnel from the water department and learn more about conservation, ecology, and the water cycle.

The Transformative-Tempered Radical: Critical

The school leaders at Millennium High School were critical transformative-tempered radicals because they embraced the idea of providing a springboard for faculty, staff, and student agency. Faculty and staff agency was facilitated by the Millennium High School administrative team.

Like so, Charles explained:

> I . . . communicate that teaching is a profession that requires inquiry and reflection, and there's always something to learn and there's always something to change about your practice—because if you're always doing the same thing, then you are limiting the potential for student learning to increase, but if you're examining your practice and really looking at areas where you can possibly improve on, then that potential for student learning to increase is always there.

Also, as a result of the student success team and division team meetings (as previously discussed in the transformational section), Charles expected his teachers to "make a difference [and consider], how am I going to change my practice as a result of those kids and the conversations that came up today [during those meetings]." In this way, to make incremental changes, the dialogue within these team meetings was pushed forward to enhance faculty, staff, and student practices.

Likewise, Dean created space for teacher agency: "I try to create space in meetings. I think we have a lot of talented people. I think sometimes it's what you don't do versus what you do. I think educators—there are way too many smart people in education, and they all have ideas and sometimes there's just not enough space or room so I just try to support [them]."

Accordingly, Yolanda said, "We really value teacher leadership. . . . We need teachers to become leaders. Anywhere from running division meetings, or acting as critical friends group coaches." Like the transformational transformative-tempered radical, by creating opportunities for faculty and staff leadership, the administrative team embraced the idea of power-with leadership strategies for incremental change at the school.

Similarly, student agency was abundant within the school. Charles noted that "we always talked about a type of agency. Students having the ability and the attitude to know that they can make change. They know how to navigate systems in order to be effective." He provided examples of opportunities for students to gain leadership experience, such as public speaking and presentations to various community partners.

Furthermore, Yolanda stated that "confidence is leadership, so when kids have confidence, they have the capacity to become leaders, and we do gateway presentations every year where every kid has to get up in front of a whole group of kids, even in ninth grade, and some kids that they don't even know very well, and talk about their learning." During my observations, I watched some seniors prepare for their gateway. During this rehearsal, seniors thematically reflected on their high school experience, using classroom artifacts from each grade level to express their academic progress and personal growth.

Lastly, the emphasis on the needs of students on an individual basis, including positive disciplinary procedures, defied the status quo. Since Dean oversaw the disciplinary actions at the school, he said, "Since I am in a role where I have to deal with behavior . . . I need to go out and find seven positive ways—if it's just saying hello in the morning and being friendly to create the feeling that the kids are liked and they are welcome here." In addition, in the first years of the school's opening, Sara explained that "we were looking at, how do we incentivize good behavior, how do we incentivize mission instead of just trying to create punitive approaches." During my observations, no punitive disciplinary actions were taken.

DISCUSSION: THE TRANSFORMATIVE-TEMPERED RADICAL ADMINISTRATIVE TEAM

The transformative-tempered radical administrative team at Millennium High School consistently use transformational and ethical, along with emerging educative and critical, leadership dimensions. In this way, they make deliberate and incremental change through their acts of leadership within the school. The transformational dimension embraces change by providing opportunities for the school community to take leadership roles. The ethical school leader recognizes power arrangements from within. The educative administrator provides the foundations for professional growth through curriculum choices and encouragement to develop leadership within the school. Finally, the critical leader supports agency and fair-mindedness among faculty, staff, and students.

First, the transformative-tempered radical leader contributes to the nurturing of school change agents by providing leadership opportunities. At the school, the student success team and division team meetings provide opportunities for faculty and staff to become school leaders. Although this leadership lacks a title, membership in these teams is honored within the school community. In part, this honor is due to the administrative team's decision to legitimize the power of the faculty and staff within these groups. Often, schools have some sort of "leadership teams." The difference at Millennium is that administrators have removed the quotation marks by believing in the decision-making power of other members of the school community.

Also, Millennium High School prides itself on building transformational, powerful relationships among the school community members. Due to the small size of the school, administrators, faculty, and staff can develop strong connections with their students. In this way, rarely does a student fall in between the cracks. If a student is experiencing a crisis, it does not go unnoticed by an adult member of the school. By building these relationships, students feel cared for. When students feel cared for, their academics will follow.

Along the same lines, parents/guardians and community members are readily included in school events. Instead of the run-of-the-mill, back-to-school night and stringent parent-teacher conferences, Millennium encourages comfort and dialogue with parents and guardians in the form of family nights and roundtables. Also, community members are always welcome at the school. Millennium works closely with community members to bring them into the school and to bring students into the community.

Second, the transformative-tempered radical school leader recognizes hierarchal power structures within the school building. To combat this structure, the leader readily utilizes open communication, professionalization, and celebrations of success. Ethical school leadership at Millennium High School entailed actively communicating with the greater school community. Phone calls, email bulletins, and social media outlets are used multiple times per week for announcements, reminders, and pictures of student accomplishments.

Also, as an act of professionalization, faculty and staff are given a certain level of autonomy inside and outside the classroom. Faculty and staff teach to the state standards while using relevant curriculum with their students. In addition, student accomplishments are highlighted weekly during whole-school meeting. Students are presented with Habits of Heart and Mind awards to highlight acts associated with these school norms.

The transformative-tempered radical administrator provides historical narratives to reveal the true nature of oppression. In this sense, oppression refers to the traditional power-over administrative practices, including leadership style, professional development, and curricular choices. Historically, school leaders ruled the school with an iron fist, and were not willing to listen and/or apply feedback from the school community. At Millennium, the leadership styles of the administrative team lend themselves to power-with community relationships.

In addition, as an educative component, the use of a critical friends group as professional development has the potential to bring a fluid, relevant, and challenging element to professional development. The choice to use project-based within place-based learning also adds depth to the school curriculum. In this way, students are aware of their imprint and capacity within their immediate surroundings.

Lastly, the transformative-tempered radical leader provides a springboard for faculty, staff, and student agency. Fair practices, such as disciplinary actions, are readily used within the school. Faculty and staff are encouraged to inquire, reflect, and expand their teaching. Similarly, the school leadership team encourages students to make a difference by providing leadership opportunities. Also at Millennium, student discipline is framed in positivity. School leaders go out of their way to find positive student attributes and incentives instead of focusing on punitive discipline.

In sum, the transformative-tempered radical administrative team at Millennium High School work together with their school stakeholders to build a nontraditional, innovative school community. Therefore, through transformative leadership practices, including transformational, ethical, educative, and critical dimensions, the administrative team at Millennium High School are tempered radicals who contribute to the dismantling of the status quo by challenging common school barriers to create a sustainable, collaborative, and inclusive charter school.

IMPLICATIONS FOR PRACTICE

The Transformative-Tempered Radical Administrator

To improve the practice of charter and traditional principals, I suggest using the stories from Millennium High School as a snapshot of what is attainable within schools. To build community, school leaders in a small or large school are encouraged to use transformative-tempered leadership practices, including transformational, ethical, educative, and critical dimensions, to enhance their school environments. Within the terms of school leadership and the use of tempered radicalism, hurried changes lead to unsustainable changes; however, tempered or steady and deliberate changes are most advantageous to school leaders and a modern school community.

Transformative-tempered radical actions enhance the education of all students and the sustainability of school community. Transformational acts, such as legitimized faculty and staff leadership teams, the building of strong student relationships, and the consistent incorporation of parents/guardians and community members, are foundational to the construction of community. Furthermore, open communication, professionalization of faculty and staff, and the celebration of student successes contribute to ethical leadership practices.

In addition, educative administrators take the time to develop the pedagogical strategies used by their faculty and staff and work to dismantle traditional curriculum to incorporate multiple ways of learning and diverse curricula. Finally, the critical leader is a catalyst for faculty, staff, and student agency. Through opportunities for inquiry and reflection, leadership within the school community builds on faculty, staff, and student personal agency.

Therefore, using Millennium High School as a model, current school leaders have the capacity to become "tempered radicals" who contribute to the building of a sustainable community, in which administrators, faculty, staff, students, parents/guardians, and community stakeholders are involved in school decision-making, events, and opportunities. As such, traditional school leadership practices are being challenged as the needs, values, and voices of the entire school community are legitimized.

NOTE

1. I realize the use of transformational to describe one of the four dimensions of the transformative leadership framework is problematic. However, the use of transformational does not refer to the Burns's (1978) theory of transformational leadership. In fact, it refers to the distinctive transformative-transformational dimension, defined as the administrative actions of transforming school practices in order to provide for equitable educational opportunities among and beyond the school community. In this way, the transformational leader contributes to the dismantling of the status quo.

REFERENCES

Burns, J. M. (1978). *Leadership*. New York: HarperCollins.
Carspecken, C. F. (1996). *Critical ethnography in educational research*. New York: Routledge.
Center for Education Reform (2016). *Choice and charter schools: Facts.* Retrieved from https://www.edreform.com/issues/choice-charter-schools/facts/
Cobb, C. D., & Glass, G. V. (1999). Ethnic segregation in Arizona charter schools. *Education Policy Analysis Archives, 7*, 1.
Dantley, M. E. (2003). Critical spirituality: Enhancing transformative leadership through critical theory and African American prophetic spirituality. *International Journal of Leadership in Education, 6*(1), 3–17.
Dixson, A. D., Royal, C., & Lawrence Henry, K. (2013). School reform and school choice. In H. R. Milner IV & K. Lomotey (Eds.), *Handbook of urban education* (pp. 474–522). New York: Routledge.
Fabricant, M., & Fine, M. (2015). *Charter schools and the corporate makeover of public education: What's at stake?* New York: Teachers College Press.
Foster, W. (1986). *Paradigms and promises*. Amherst, NY: Prometheus Books.
Foster, W. (1988). Educational administration: A critical appraisal. In D. E. Griffiths & R. T. Stout (Eds.), *Leaders for America's schools: The report and papers of the National Commission on Excellence in Educational Administration* (pp. 68–82). New York: McCutchan.
Foster, W. (1989). The administrator as a transformative intellectual. *Peabody Journal of Education, 66*(3), 5–18.
Freire, P. (1970). *Pedagogy of the oppressed*. New York: Continuum International.
Glesne, C. (2011). *Becoming qualitative researchers: An introduction* (4th ed.). Boston: Pearson.
Huerta, L. A., & Zuckerman, A. (2009). An institutional theory analysis of charter schools: Addressing institutional challenges to scale. *Peabody Journal of Education, 84*(3), 414–431.
Lubienski, C. A., & Weitzel, P. C. (2010). Two decades of charter schools. In C. A. Lubienski and P. C. Weitzel (Eds.), *The charter school experiment: Expectations, evidence, and implications* (pp. 2–14). Cambridge, MA: Harvard Education Press.
Madison, D. S. (2012). *Critical ethnography: Method, ethics, and performance*. Los Angeles: Sage.
Maxwell, J. A. (2013). *Qualitative research design: An interactive approach*. Los Angeles: Sage.
Meier, D. (2002). *In schools we trust: Creating communities of learning in an era of testing and standardization*. Boston: Beacon Press.
Meyerson, D. E. (2003). *Tempered radicals: How everyday leaders inspire change at work*. Boston: Harvard Business School Press.
Sass, T. R. (2006). Charter schools and student achievement in Florida. *Education, 1*(1), 91–122.
Shields, C. M. (2010a). Transformative leadership: Working for equity in diverse contexts. *Educational Administration Quarterly, 46*(4), 558–589.
Shields, C. M. (2010b). Leadership: Transformative. *International Encyclopedia of Education, 5*, 26–33.
Shanker, A. (1988). Convention plots new course—A charter for change. *New York Times*, July 10.
Vergari, S. (1999) Charter schools: A primer on the issues. *Education and Urban Society, 31*(4), 389–405.
Weiner, E. J. (2003). Secretary Paulo Freire and the democratization of power: Toward a theory of transformative leadership. *Educational Philosophy and Theory, 35*(1), 89–106.

Chapter Six

Conclusion

Confirming and Expanding an Understanding of the Charter Principalship

Dana L. Bickmore and Marytza A. Gawlik

The purpose in organizing this book was to add to the limited research that has explored and described the work of charter school principals. To this end, contributing researchers employed qualitative research methods to provide rich and nuanced descriptions of principal leadership in charter schools in a variety of contexts across various states. The authors in this volume have confirmed themes that have permeated the literature surrounding the charter principal. Additionally, through multiple descriptions of the charter principal's work, authors have expanded on these themes.

Authors have also highlighted topics related to the work of charter principals that have not been fully investigated in the literature. These topics have implication for practice and further study. This chapter provides a review of these collective themes and topics that have emerged from the research described in this book to support and better understand the charter principalship.

CONFIRMING THE LITERATURE

Three themes have permeated the limited research and literature focused on charter principal leadership. First, charter principals are afforded autonomy and flexibility to lead and manage schools (Gawlik, 2008; Wohlstetter, Smith, & Farrell, 2013). Second, charter principals should and do focus on the mission and vision of the school (Dressler, 2001; Merseth, 2009). Third, the charter principalship requires engaging in additional management and instructional tasks beyond those of traditional principals (Campbell, Gross, & Lake, 2008). The specific examples within the chapters of this book confirm these themes, but also describe how charter principals engage in leadership across these themes.

Charter Principal Autonomy

Each author in this book, in some fashion, discussed the autonomy and flexibility garnered by charter principals. There was a clear consensus that charter principals had a great deal of autonomy to lead and manage their schools. As in previous research, charter principals exercised their autonomy in direct and indirect ways to support the school mission and the principals' vision and goals for the school.

Of particular note was the charter principal's direct and intentional involvement in human resource management. Whether during start-up or as the charter developed, principals were highly engaged in hiring staff and setting high expectations for teacher engagement in schools and with students. As Cannata and colleagues (chapter 2) suggest, the most important task in which charter principals engage is staffing. Although traditional principals may prioritize human resource management, chapter authors described a level of involvement in managing staff only possible because of the autonomy afforded the charter principal, such as swift termination of staff.

In congruence with past research, the authors described charter principals using their autonomy to develop and change school structures, policies, and processes to the extent not normally given traditional principals. Descriptions of founding principals' use of autonomy encompassed detailed planning of school structure and policy. Examples of developing school processes included how principals engaged board members and established procedures for guiding teacher and student interactions.

Authors also provided rich descriptions of how principals used their autonomy after the initial founding to adjust and change policies and procedures. Although most authors described how principals used their autonomy judiciously to make incremental changes to structures, policies, and procedures, there were examples of how charter principals have the discretion to make quick and radical changes. For traditional principals, both incremental and radical decisions generally require approval and, often, district policy changes.

Charter Principals and Mission

Also in alignment with the current charter principal literature, research described in these chapters illustrated the importance of charter principals focusing their decisions on a clearly defined mission. Successful charter schools appear to begin with principals who can articulate and make mission the center of all decisions. Authors provided strong examples of how principals who focused on a unique, student-centered mission led to innovative schools that met student needs. In contrast, evidence surfaced suggesting charter principals who do not prioritize the intent and unique elements of the chartering mission may negatively affect school culture and potential school outcomes.

Charter Principals and Additional Tasks

In every chapter, authors provided examples of tasks performed by principals that may not be expected of traditional school principals, confirming the volume and complexity of the charter principalship in the current literature. In these settings, principals took on tasks such as managing budgets and buildings, finding funding to meet management and instructional priorities, and setting policies that met the needs and demands of authorizer, parents, and students. Charter principals in these chapters navigated these tasks in various ways, confirming that context makes a difference in the work of the charter principal, as it does for traditional principals (Goldring, Huff, May, & Camburn, 2008).

NUANCED LOOKS AT CHARTER PRINCIPAL LEADERSHIP

Beyond confirming previous themes surrounding the charter principal, the research described in these chapters also highlighted the interplay of autonomy with school culture, mission, and change. The importance of a collaborative and healthy culture and climate has been a topic of traditional principal research. Researchers conclude that the principal is key to developing and maintaining a culture that can positively impacts student outcomes (Hoy & Hannum, 1997; Louis et al., 2010). Little research, however, exists regarding the relationship between charter principal autonomy and school culture.

The authors in this text addressed how charter principals used their autonomy to develop and maintain culture. Authors pointed to the need for charter principals to use their autonomy to develop a collaborative and healthy climate and culture that could support the overall vision and mission of the school. Cannata and colleagues (chapter 2) concluded that second to hiring staff, building a positive culture is the most important task for establishing an effective charter school. Walls and colleagues (chapter 3), supported by DeMartino (chapter 5), described how principals who developed a positive culture, in which staff and students felt valued and cared for, were able to support the overall mission of the school.

In juxtaposition, Bickmore (chapter 4) exposed how the extended autonomy given a charter principal led to a culture and climate that was negative and replaced the original mission of the school. Using the power of autonomy, the principal made unilateral decisions rather than developing a collaborative culture and positive climate. Autonomy appears to be a double-edged sword that can be wielded for negative outcomes as well as positive. What makes the difference? Are the mechanisms for developing and maintaining culture the same as with traditional principals, or does the ability to make quick and rapid changes require a new understanding of leadership and culture?

The interplay of charter principal leadership, change, and stability also surfaced in several chapters. Innovation and improved equitable access to quality education were two original goals of the charter school movement, and continue to be prominent reasons for support of charter schools (Weitzel & Lubienski, 2010). In support of these two goals, charter principals in diverse settings are tasked with leading schools that perform as laboratories of innovation and equity.

Walls, Ryu, and Johnson (chapter 3) and DeMartino (chapter 5) documented how charter principals acted as change agents to create unique schools that met the needs of the students from diverse backgrounds in equitable ways. However, these authors described how charter principals moved to stabilize their schools, limiting radical change and innovations to more effectively align with their school's mission and goals in order to meet student needs. Once schools were up and running, principals appeared less concerned about innovations and change than stability that could lead to goal attainment.

Bickmore (chapter 4) provided an alternate description of a charter principal that was in a continuous change mode, using radical changes over an extended period as a means to meet goals and improve student outcomes in a high-impact school. This continuous attempt to innovate and change appeared to be less effective than the results obtained by those charter principals who moved change forward incrementally.

DeMartino (chapter 5) presents a conceptual framework for and an example of charter leadership that may provide charter principals with a guidepost to meet policy intentions of innovation and equity, while effectively meeting specific school goals and student needs. Charter principals in this framework use the power of autonomy to value and empower the school community, develop ethical and collaborative relations across the community to meet needs, and support collaborative efforts to dismantle inequitable practices through deliberate and incremental negotiations and actions.

Rather than using the autonomy afforded charter principals to make radical change, the charter principal employs an incremental change process: "[H]urried changes lead to unsustainable changes; however, tempered or steady and deliberate changes are most advantageous to school leaders and a modern school community" (DeMartino, this book, p. 88). Although the charter principals may have the autonomy to make radical, rapid changes, within the framework of transformative tempered radicalism, charter principals employ engaging, deliberate, shared, and empowering change as a more effective leadership path.

The relationship between charter principals' use of autonomy and school-level change, innovation, and culture needs further investigation. The traditional school literature indicates collaborative and distributive leadership are more effective in supporting student outcomes (Hoy & Hannum, 1997). More studies need to occur to determine how charter principals balance the power of autonomy to make unilateral decisions and the push for innovation with the development of collaborative, stable school cultures.

IMPLICATION FOR PRACTICE

The chapters in this book, individually and collectively, provide charter principals with rich descriptions of how charter leaders across the United States engaged in their work. Charter school leadership, as described in this text, certainly has similarities to traditional school leadership, but this book provides nuanced descriptions of the charter principalship. Charter principals are encouraged to examine how their own work and context compare to the work and context of school leaders described within each chapter.

We suggest charter principals reflect on how they use autonomy, support school mission, and prioritize their tasks. Each school described in these chapters was unique, largely because of the principals' enactment of autonomy to prioritize tasks that supported the designated mission. Principals reading these chapters should compare and contrast their own context and work to glean how best to lead their schools in regard to autonomy, mission, and the complexity of tasks required of the charter principalship. Context matters, so the chapters presented here are not blueprints for principals to copy, but rather multiple guideposts to triangulate a course of action.

Charter principals may also interrogate their own practice in relationship to building and sustaining culture and engaging in change and innovation. Principals reading the descriptions of school administrators in this text should reflect on the examples and non-examples presented. Principals should strongly consider the pace of change and implementation of innovations in relationship to school culture. The authors in these chapters provide examples of how charter principals used their autonomy both for radical and tempered change that had important impacts on school culture. Charter principals should consider the tension between collaboratively building culture and using autonomy unilaterally for rapid changes.

Those supporting charter principals, such as boards, charter management organizations, and state organizations, may use descriptions of the charter principal's work outlined within this book to formulate how they can support principals. Chapter authors provide details of the volume and complexities of tasks and responsibilities experienced by charter principals as they lead schools. The complex and varied roles and tasks of the charter principal highlight the need for additional support, including preparation and professional development specific to charter leadership.

For researchers, there is continued need to explore autonomy, mission alignment, and the additional tasks required of charter principals. This is particularly true of the interactions of autonomy in different state contexts and across governance structures, such as charter school networks and nonprofit and for-profit charter management organizations. Additionally, researchers should consider how context affects principals' tasks and task completion.

Researchers also need to examine specific leadership topics and skills. Beyond further investigation of culture building, researchers should explore how charter principals deal with such leadership skills as conflict resolution, decision-making, and time management. Researchers can explore a plethora of specific topics that may provide charter principals with ideas and solutions to better lead in a context that is different from the traditional principal.

Frameworks and theories that can both guide and explain the work of charter principals from a more global perspective are required as well. There is a need to know if current frameworks and theories associated with traditional principal leadership are applicable to the charter context. DeMartino, in this text, suggested a framework that may be applicable for charter principal leadership, but this framework needs further exploration.

A primary intent of charter school policies is to provide greater latitude and autonomy to those that lead these organizations (Weitzel & Lubienski, 2010). The authors in this text provide policy makers with real accounts of how autonomy affects the work of charter principals, as well as how charter principals are using the autonomy afforded them within schools. Policy makers should use these real accounts of charter principal leadership to evaluate and adjust charter policies to support charter principals in their efforts to serve parents and students.

There is every indication that U.S. educational policy will continue to promote charter schooling as an option within the public education system. With the critical role of the principal in organization viability and student success, it is important to understand how the charter school principal engages in leadership. The authors in this text offered a granular look at the charter principalship, such that charter principals, charter organizations, researchers, and policy makers may examine their own practices. Our hope is that this text will spark further dialogue and investigations into the vital work of charter principals, with the ultimate goal of improving the lives of students.

REFERENCES

Campbell, C., Gross, B., & Lake, R. (2008). The high-wire job of charter school principalship. *Education Week, 28*(3), 56–58.

Dressler, B. (2001). Charter school leadership. *Education and Urban Society, 33*(2), 15.

Gawlik, M. A. (2008). Breaking loose: Principal autonomy in charter and public schools. *Educational Policy, 22*(6), 783–804.

Goldring, E., Huff, J., May, H., & Camburn, E. (2008). School context and individual characteristics: What influences principal practice? *Journal of Educational Administration, 46*(3), 332–352. doi:10.1108/0957823081086927

Hoy, W. K., & Hannum, J. W. (1997). Middle school climate: An empirical assessment of organizational health and student achievement. *Educational Administration Quarterly, 33*(3), 290–311.

Louis, K. S., Leithwood, K., Wahlstrom, K. L., Anderson, S. E., Michlin, M., Gordon, M., et al. (2010). *Learning from leadership: Investigating the links to improved student learning: Final report of research findings*. Minneapolis and Toronto: Wallace Foundation. Retrieved from http://www.wallacefoundation.org/knowledge-center/Documents/Investigating-the-Links-to-Improved-Student-Learning.pdf

Merseth, K. K. (2009). *Inside urban charter schools*. Cambridge, MA: Harvard Education Press.

Weitzel, P. C. , & Lubienski, C. A. (2010). Grading charter schools: Access, innovation, and competition. In C. A. Lubienski & P. C. Weitzel (Eds.), *The charter school experiment: Expectations, evidence, and implications* (pp. 15–32). Cambridge, MA: Harvard Education Press.

Wohlstetter, P., Smith, J., & Farrell, C. (2013). *Choices and challenges: Charter school performance in perspective*. Cambridge, MA: Harvard Education Press.

Index

accountability, 1, 11–12, 29
achievement data, state, 13
achievement effects, vii
African American students, 2, 49. *See also* black students
after-school program, 50, 60, 63
American Educational Research Association, xi
Arizona, 2, 13
at-risk students, 1, 49
autonomy, 2, 11, 91, 92

Battistich, Victor, 31
behavior management system, 36
belonging, student sense of, 40, 41, 43, 44, 45
black(s), 14
board members: founding, 14; principals and, 19–20, 92
bonuses. *See* rewards
budget management, 9, 12, 22
buildings, school, 24–25
business functions, xii
business manager, 22
business operations, 13, 22–25

California, 2, 12
caring, 42, 44; basis of, 30; Cedarlane Academy and, 39, 40, 42, 45; characteristics of, 30, 31; communities and, 31; cultural differences, 31, 32; engagement and, 33; familial, 30, 31; organizational, 30; schools and, 31–32
Carspecken, C. F., 77, 78
Cedarlane Academy, xii, 30; active supervision in, 36; caring culture, 40, 42, 45; collaboration at, 38, 43, 45; cultural differences within, 43; finances and, 38; founding of, 35; immigrant students in, 36, 43; leaders of, 35–37, 43, 44, 45; methods of, 33; school climate in, 36; students, 29, 30, 31, 33, 34, 40–42, 43; teachers at, 36–37
Charter Management Organizations (CMOs), 7n1, 72, 73
The Charter School Dust-Up, vii
charter support organizations (CSOs), 13, 17; board members and, 19, 20; building acquisition and, 24, 25; business management and, 22; decision making and, 17; principal responsibilities and, 18; resources and, 24; school mission and, 26
Clark, Mr., Kids Korner and, 55, 56–67, 68–69
collaboration: Cedarlane Academy and, 38, 43, 45; community, 74; core values and, 15, 69; curriculum choice and, 38; Kids Korner and, 67, 69; transformational leadership and, 52
Colorado, 13

99

community-based institutions (CBIs), 72, 73
community-driven schools, 72
contemporary charter school, 73, 74
critical friends group (CFG), 84
culture differences, 29, 31, 32, 37, 42, 43, 44
culture, school, xii, 50, 54; Cedarlane Academy, 43; embedding mechanisms, 53; goal attainment and, 50, 51, 52; at Kids Korner, 49, 50, 57–67; leadership and, 51–54; mature, 53; mechanisms of, 53; midlife, 53; organization's, 50, 52; student success and, 51; types of, 52
curriculum: charter school, 73; International Baccalaureate, 38, 39, 42; localism and, viii

data-driven instruction, 63
dean, school, 41
discipline, at Kids Korner, 60, 64
district reforms, 2
division team meetings, 80, 85, 86

Educational Delusions, vii
educational management organizations (EMOs), 7n1, 73
engagement: culture of, 32, 33; strategies, 32
Envoy nonverbal behavior management system, 36
ethics, transformative leadership and, 76, 82–83, 86
evidence-based strategies, 29
extended day program. *See* after-school program
external policy expectations, viii

facilities, 9, 24
family night, 82, 86
finance committee, 23
financial accounting, 23
financial director, 22
financial budget management, 12
first generation charter schools, 1
Florida, 2, 13
food service, 17
for-profit charter schools, 11
for-profit management, 50

founders: budget and, 24; building locations and, 24–25; business operation management, 22–23; challenges of, 11–13; classroom experience of, 17; decision-making and, 17; facilities and, 24–25; mission and, 15, 16; outsourcing and, 23

gateway presentation, 85
gender data, 14–15
Georgia, 13
goals: culture, 50, 51, 52; "golden ticket" and, 64–65; principal's, 94; school, 92
"golden tickets," 64–66
governing board, 12, 19, 23; charter school, 12, 20; continuity of, 21; principal succession procedures and, 21; responsibilities of, 19–20

Habit of Heart and Mind, 83, 87
Henig, Jeffrey, 3, 11
Hill, Charles, 78, 80, 82, 84, 85
Hispanic students, 14

immigrant students, xii, 29, 30, 33, 36
instructional coach, 55, 57, 59, 60, 62, 63, 64, 65, 66
instructional dean, 19, 23
instructional program, designing, 9
International Baccalaureate (IB) curriculum, 33, 38, 39, 42
interviews, 33–34; administrator, 34, 35–37; student, 36, 40–43, 44; teacher, 35, 38–39

Kids Korner Charter School, 49, 54; changing principal at, 54; collaboration at, 67, 69; culture at, 49, 50, 57–67; data sources, 55; discipline at, 60, 64; instructional coach at, 55, 57, 59, 60, 62, 63, 64, 65, 66; mission of, 49, 50; Mr. Clark at, 55, 56–67; parents and, 50, 59; principal of, 50; teachers at, 49, 50, 55, 57, 58, 59, 60, 61–67
Knowledge Is Power Program (KIPP), 18

laws, local, 9, 11, 20
leadership, xii; culture development and, 51–54; transformational, 52;

transitions, 20–21
location, school, 24
Louisiana, 2, 13
low socioeconomic communities, 72
lunch program, reduced-price, students, 4, 11, 49

market-oriented charter schools, 11
Michigan, 13
Millennium High School, xii, 71, 88; administration team at, 86–87; cell phones at, 83; cofounders, 78, 79, 79–80; community and, 82, 86, 87; culture at, 81; curriculum, 82, 84, 87; development of, 78–79; disciplinary procedures at, 85, 87; division team meetings at, 80, 85, 86; ethics at, 76, 82–83, 86, 87; faculty, 79, 84, 85, 87; family night at, 82, 86; gateway presentation at, 85; Habits of Heart and Mind at, 83, 87; location, 78; opening of, 78; parents and, 82, 86; place-based learning at, 84, 87; project-based learning at, 84, 87; race and, 79; size of, 81; staff, 79, 83, 84, 85, 87; student(s), 79, 80, 81, 83, 85; student success team at, 80; student voice committee at, 83; teachers at, 79, 84, 85; transformative leadership at, 74, 80; transformative-tempered radicals at, 84; trust and, 82
Minnesota, 1
mission, xii; core, 14, 15, 16; decision making and, 15; establishing school, 11, 13, 17; of Kids Korner, 49, 50; leadership and, 52, 53; principal and, 26, 91, 94, 95
mission-driven organization, 26
mission-oriented charter schools, 11, 17
multicultural schools, 29–30. *See also* immigrant students; Muslim students
multidisciplinary leaders, viii
Muslim students, 37, 42

New Orleans, ix, 2
New York, 13
No Child Left Behind, 29
Noddings, Nel, 30–31
nonprofit: charter organization, 73; management, 50; schools, 11

office manager, 22
Ohio, 13
organizations, 50; charter schools as innovation, 51; culture and, 50, 51; dysfunctional, 54; environment changes and, 53; midlife, 53; subcultures, 53; technology and, 54
outsourcing services, 23

paraprofessionals, 50
parents: Cedarlane Academy and, 35, 37; charter schools and, 16; Kids Korner, 50, 59; Millenium High School, 82, 86
Payne, Charles, 3
photo-elicitation, 33, 40, 41
photographs, student, 33, 34, 40, 41, 42
place-based learning, 84, 87
power-over leadership, 71, 74, 77, 82, 87
power-with strategies, 71, 74
principal, xii, 26; autonomy, 91, 92, 93, 94, 95; board members and, 19–20, 92; business management and, 22–24, 25–26; characteristics of, 5–6; charter support organizations and, 18; culture and, 19, 95; first, 9–26; founding, 14; global perspective of, 96; importance of, 3–4; Kids Korner, 50; leadership, 3, 4–5; management, 91, 92; mission and, 26, 91, 94, 95; networking and, 18; public school, 11; role of, 5–6; school changes and, 94, 95; school culture and, 93; school goals and, 94; school mission and, 91, 93, 95; school structure and, 92; second, 21; staff and, 18, 19, 92; student learning and, 10, 19; tasks of, 18, 20, 93, 96; traditional, 5, 10, 54, 74, 88, 92, 93, 95, 96; transformative tempered radicalism and, 95; transitions, 20–21, 25–26; turnover rates, 10
privatization, 2
professional development, 4, 10, 22–23, 58, 59, 87
project-based learning, 14, 84, 87
public school: comparison to, vii, viii, 1, 12, 72; impact on, vii; integration of, 3; principals, 11; resistance in, 72

race: caring forms and, 31; data, 14, 15; Millennium High School and, 79
Race to the Top, 29
Ravitch, Diane, 2, 3
reduced price lunch students, 4, 14, 49
refugee students, 17. *See also* immigrant students
research, 33–34, 91, 96
resources, 13, 24

Saturday School, 60, 63
Schein, Edgar H., 50, 52, 53
school(s): calendar, 37, 45; caring in, 31–32; community demographics of, 78–79; engagement dimensions in, 32–33; founding, xii; International Baccalaureate curriculum in, 33, 35, 38, 39, 42; non-profit, 11; second generation, 1; transformative leadership and, 76, 77
The School Choice Wars, vii
segregation, charter school, 73
Shanker, Albert, 72
Smith, Dean, 79, 82, 83, 85
South Carolina, 13
special education students, 1
staff, hiring of, 18, 19
state policies, for charter schools, 51
student(s), viii; achievement growth, 13; at-risk, 40; caring and, 40, 45; Cedarlane Academy, 29, 30, 31, 33, 34, 40–42, 43; engagement, xii, 32–33; Habit of Heart and Mind, 83; immigrant, 29, 30, 33; International Baccalaureate curriculum and, 33; interviews, 36, 40–43, 44; Kids Korner, 59, 60, 62, 63–64; learning experiences of, 10; low-income, 16; lunch program for, 4, 11, 49; marginalized, 74; Millennium High School, 79, 80, 81, 83, 85; peers of, 41; photo-elicitation and, 33, 40, 41; photographs and, 33, 34, 40, 41, 42; recruitment, 11; relationships, 81; school environment and, 19, 40–42; school leaders and, 41; student success team (SST), 80, 85, 86; teacher cultural differences and, 43; teacher relationships and, 40–41

Teach for America, 56, 63, 66
teacher(s), 10, 29, 30; assistants, 61, 63; autonomy of, 1; caring and, 31; Cedarlane Academy, 36–37, 38–39, 43; collaboration, 38; criticism of, 37; cultural differences and, 43; engagement and, 33; excommunication of, 61, 62, 64, 65, 67; "golden tickets" and, 64–67; hiring of, 11, 18, 19; International Baccalaureate curriculum and, 38, 39, 42; interviews, 35, 38–39; Kids Korner, 49, 50, 55, 57, 58, 59, 60, 61, 62–64, 65–67; Millennium High School, 79, 84, 85, 87; paraprofessionals and, 50; professional development of, 4, 58, 59, 87; retirement, 63, 66; rewards for, 64, 65, 67; school mission and, 11; staff support for, 43–44; student relationships and, 40–41; turnover, 36
technical assistance, 13
tempered radicalism, 74; overview of, 77; transformative, 80
Tennessee, 13
Texas, 2
third generation charter schools, 2
Thomas, Sara, 72, 78, 79, 81, 82, 83, 85–86
time management, 18
traditional principals, 5, 10, 54, 74, 88, 92, 93, 95, 96
training support, 13
transformational dimension, administrative, 75
transformational-tempered strategies, 80, 82, 88
transformative leadership, 71, 72; community attributes and, 75; critical dimension and, 76, 84–85, 87, 88; educative dimension and, 76, 84, 87, 88; empirical review of, 74–75; environment and, 75; ethical dimension and, 76, 82, 83, 87, 88; school community and, 76, 77; strategies of, 80, 82; tempered radicalism and, 77, 80; theoretical framework, 75–76; theory, 75; transformative-tempered radical team and, 86–87

transformative leadership practices, xii, 74–75
Tronto, J. C., 30
turnover rates, principal, 10

Units of Inquiry, 39, 42
urban area schools, 2
U.S. educational policy, charter school, 96

Valenzuela, Angela, 31, 32, 33, 43
Vergari, S., 72
vision: founders', 13; principals', 91, 92

Washington, DC, 2, 13
Wright, Yolanda, 71, 78, 79, 81, 84, 85

About the Editors

Dana L. Bickmore is an associate professor in the Educational Policy and Leadership program at the University of Nevada, Las Vegas. Her research explores principal leadership in middle and charter schools. This work is informed by her years in public education as a teacher, principal, and district administrator. Dr. Bickmore has authored numerous research articles examining school principal leadership.

Marytza A. Gawlik is an assistant professor in the Educational Leadership and Policy Studies department at Florida State University. Dr. Gawlik's research examines various aspects of charter schools, including leadership, accountability, autonomy, succession, and socialization. Her work spans a decade, and she has authored several research articles related to charter school leadership and policy.

www.ingramcontent.com/pod-product-compliance
Lightning Source LLC
Chambersburg PA
CBHW020752230426
43665CB00009B/567